T0114754

Sangaya

First Published by Kachere Series in 1996 and 1999 (revised).
This 3rd edition unchanged from 1999.

Published by
Luviri Press
P/Bag 201 Luwinga
Mzuzu 2

ISBN   978-99960-98-28-4
eISBN   978-99960-98-29-1

Biographies of People and Parishes no. 1

Luviri Press is represented outside Malawi by:
African Books Collective Oxford (order@africanbookscollective.com)

www.mzunipress.blogspot.com
www.africanbookscollective.com

Sangaya

Silas S. Ncozana

Luviri Press

Biographies of People and Parishes no. 1

Mzuzu

2018

Biographies of People and Parishes

There have been a good number of solid monographs and other major books on Malawian Church History, written over many decades. A good number of them are still in print, and others will be made available again in the Luviri Classics and Luviri Reprint Series. Over the same period many smaller books were published, starting with autobiographies of early Malawian church leaders and a history, in Chichewa, of Blantyre Mission and its Beginnings. Over the decades, more such little books were written, be it biographies of church leaders or of a congregation. They are not of the academic rigour of a monograph, but they do contain information that is available nowhere else. This series is to make them available again, not only in Malawi, where many of them have been published, but also worldwide through the Print on Demand system of the African Books Collective, which represents Luviri Press outside Malawi.

This series will also attempt to publish unpublished manuscripts that fit the remit of this series. These maybe manuscripts of old, but also recent research on the history of peoples and parishes (and also of Christian institutions). If you have any manuscript to propose, contact the editors, under luviripress1@gmail.com.

The Editors

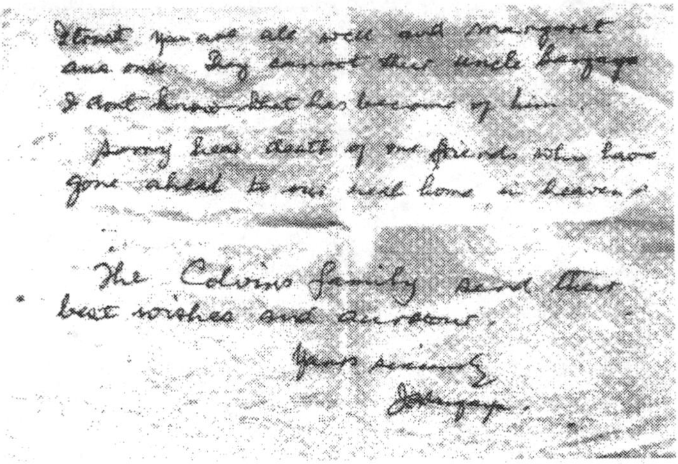

I trust you are all well and Margaret and ones. Say [illegible] their uncle Sangaya. I don't know what has become of him.

Sorry [illegible] death of our friends who have gone ahead to our real home in heaven.

The Colvins family send their best wishes and au revoir.

Yours sincerely

J. Sangaya.

Letter written by Sangaya to the author dated 28 June 1975

Contents

Preface

The Very Rev. Jonathan Sangaya served the Synod of Blantyre of the Church of Central Africa Presbyterian from 1927 to 1979, the year he died. He initially served the Synod as a school teacher in one of its mission schools from 1927 to 1945. In 1943 Sangaya left teaching in order to join the Army. As a soldier he was sent to East Africa where he was stationed for three years. When Sangaya returned to Malawi after the war, he rejoined the mission as a teacher. In 1948, he began training for the ministry of Word and Sacrament, and in 1952 he was ordained. In 1962 Sangaya became the first Malawian General Secretary for the Synod of Blantyre. In the same year, he was also elected Moderator of the General Synod of the Church of Central Africa Presbyterian.

No one can adequately assess the tremendous impact that Sangaya made upon the Synod of Blantyre. As a teacher, pastor, administrator, preacher, ecumenist and internationalist, his contribution to the life and work of the Synod of Blantyre was widespread and far-reaching. Under his leadership the Synod developed considerably as an indigenous church which began giving expression to Christianity in a uniquely African way. As well, important service organs of the church, such as the Christian Service Committee of the churches in Malawi, Chilema Lay Training Centre, the Private Hospital Association of Malawi, and Theological Education by Extension in Malawi (TEEM), came

Blantyre Mission, August 1978. Left to right: Rev. J.D. Sangaya, Rev. Morton Taylor, the author, Rev. C. B. Simuja

into being as a result of Sangaya's initiative and leadership. Corporate work among Protestant Christians of various traditions was also enriched by the efforts he made to strengthen the work of the Christian Council of Malawi. Indeed, Sangaya dedicated his whole life to the proclamation of the Christian faith and the effect of his leadership is still felt by many of us.

10

Now Sangaya is no longer with us. He is survived by his widow, Christian Sangaya, and two daughters, Fanny and Eleanor. Sangaya is also survived by many memories as well.

My heart and head are full of the recollections I have of him. I first met Sangaya in 1961 when I was a Form 1 student at Henry Henderson Institute (HHI). At that time he had just returned from Scotland, where he had gone to study administration, and he therefore spoke English with a Scottish accent. His personal charm came across to me in his soft voice which invited me to sit down and tell him all that I had to say. I was responsible for organising morning prayers at the HHI Secondary School. I explained to Sangaya that I had come to invite him to conduct a morning service of worship during the school assembly. He accepted the invitation, showing a rapt interest in the subject. He encouraged me to come again and see him if I ever needed any help. Sangaya was a big man in stature, and he was a character of forbidding reputation. I had heard about him before from fellow students and teachers. I had also heard about him from my relations and neighbours. Further, I had heard him speak over the radio and had seen his photographs in newspapers. I was glad to have met him in person at that time. Little did I know that Sangaya would later be my workmate and mentor.

Fifteen years later, I was privileged to work as Deputy General Secretary during Sangaya's last four years of life. I recall with fondness how frequently he used the expression "Tigawane", "Let's share", whenever he brought meat, or when he had read something important. (Meat is always cheaper outside town than inside town, so when one goes on a trip, one buys good cheap meat.) But the sharing spirit in Sangaya was not limited to a few people. It extended to all.

I remember his impressive build, his loud laughter and the peculiar way his forehead would be creased when he was displeased. I learned a great deal from him and I often recall the things he taught me and the advice he offered me. His outstanding ability to listen, to take everyone seriously and to make sound decisions gave him a capacity for leadership which I did not fully appreciate until he was gone. He truly was a leader of our own hearts. This view, I am sure, is shared by all who knew and loved him.

Therefore, in this book we remember with affection a man who was an authentic Christian and a strong administrator, a man who made a vast contribution to the Church of Jesus Christ in general and in particular to the life and work of the Synod of Blantyre - the church he loved and lived his life for.

Let us praise God then for this great churchman and let us rejoice that we have such a rich heritage today because of the way in which Sangaya toiled so diligently to cultivate it for us.

Acknowledgements

Writing this book has been possible because of the support and encouragement of numerous friends.

Foremost, I would like to thank Mrs C. Sangaya, the widow of the late Very Rev. J.D. Sangaya, and the late McNeil Sangaya, their first-born son, who sat with me for many hours answering my questions about the "Old Man", as Jonathan Douglas Sangaya was affectionately referred to by family and friends. Indeed, I am indebted to the entire Sangaya family for their cooperation, encouragement and interest in the writing of this book.

My appreciation goes to the Rev. Tom and Mrs Patsy Colvin for sharing their invaluable personal knowledge about the life of J.D. Sangaya. The information they gave me added much to the richness of this book. I am also indebted to many ex Malawian missionaries who gave me valuable information about Sangaya.

At various stages of the manuscript of this book, Clara Henderson read it and gave helpful criticism that helped to shape this book. To her I say, "Zikomo".

May I also thank the Synod of Blantyre of the CCAP for the interest it has shown in this project.

The time I took to write this book was in the evenings, time precious to my family. Therefore I want to specially thank Margaret, my wife, and our children Samuel, Davie, Joe, Chimwe and Farai for their patience and moral support.

I also thank the Princeton Theological Seminary in the USA, where I finally completed writing the book, for giving me comfortable accommodation from 29th August 1994 to March 1995. Last and not least, I wish to thank Rev. Jack M. Bowers for proofreading and typing the final script of the first edition.

S.S. Ncozana

His Family Background

The family of the Very Rev. Jonathan D. Sangaya came into being out of two different traditions, namely the Ngoni and the Yao. The Ngoni of Ntcheu District, from where Douglas Mzangaya Dzonzi, Jonathan's father, came, were part of a large body which settled in Malawi about 1864. The Ngoni came from South Africa where they were part of the Zulu ethnic group, which are well known in history for their stamina and warring habits.

The Yao of Chiradzulu, the birthplace of Jonathan's mother, Che Fanny Pambalipe (meaning "the one who ignites grass"), trace their history back to Mozambique. Che Fanny had Lomwe blood, possibly from her mother's side. The information on this point is not clear. However, the Yao, unlike the Ngoni who entered Malawi in regiments, came into the country in families. They are noted in history for their active engagement in the slave trade. They acted as middlemen between Arabs on the coast and the African chiefs in the interior. Bridglal Pachai has covered much of the history of the Ngoni and the Yao people in his book, *Malawi: The History of the Nation* (London: Longman, 1973).

The marriage between Douglas Nzangaya and Che Fanny Pambalipe was significant. It marked the fact that Malawi, then Nyasaland, was undergoing radical social change. Ethnic barriers were crumbling, intermarriage was on the increase, and more people were travelling long distances. Before this period, marriages between people of different ethnic groups were, in normal circumstances, rare. Marriage had to be within one's ethnic group, and among cousins. This was especially true among the Yao. Therefore when Douglas Mzangaya Dzonzi, a Ngoni man, and Che Fanny Pambalipe, a Yao woman, married, it was as if two different worlds had come together.

The name "Mzangaya" is the uncorrupted name by which Sangaya was known at Bawi village in the Ntcheu district. "Dzonzi" was Mzangaya's clan name. In about 1890, Mzangaya Dzonzi left Bawi as a *mtengatenga*, a load carrier. When his party arrived in Blantyre, he slipped away from his masters and took refuge at the Blantyre Mission. There the Yao of the area could not pronounce the "Mz". Instead of two consonants, they put an "S" and Mzangaya became Sangaya. When he became a Christian, he was baptized under the new name, Douglas Sangaya. At the Mission Mzangaya was employed by Mr A. Currie as a "kitchen boy" and later promoted to the position of cook. Currie was one of the Scottish missionaries at Blantyre Mission responsible for the maintenance of buildings. It was during his time at Blantyre Mission that Mzangaya married Che Fanny Pambalipe.

Douglas Mzangaya Dzonzi and his wife Che Fanny first lived on the east bank of Mudi stream near the present Masauto Chiphembere Highway and Mandala Fork Road. There Jonathan Douglas Sangaya was born on 31st October, 1907. However, after a brief period of time along Mudi stream, they were moved to Njamba, due to the expansion of the town of Blantyre.

Njamba lies at about 975 metres above sea level. It is located near Soche Mountain, in the middle of three hills, Soche, Michiru and Ndirande. The area has a beautiful temperate climate. This whole area was Chief Kapeni's country and was densely populated. Here in this area the young Sangaya grew up. In about 1947, the Mzangaya family had to move away from Njamba in a mass exodus, to give way to the still growing town of Blantyre. They settled in Ntenjela, about 15 kilometres north of Blantyre. There both Douglas and Che Fanny Mzangaya died. They were buried in the church graveyard at Ntenjela.

Douglas Mzangaya had lived a quiet life. As a Christian, he loved to go to church, and if illness did not hold him back, he attended church services every Sunday. When the young Jonathan was old enough to walk, he often went to the church with his father. Frequenting the church exposed him to the Christian faith early in his life.

Jonathan was the firstborn of four children. Emmie, Ethelo and Margaret followed. As Jonathan was the first born and the only son, he received special favours from his mother and father. They bought him good clothes, and he always had the advantage of eating meat specially kept for him by his mother. Among the Ngoni people, meat is a treat, which is why his mother would save him some. Consequently, his sisters were jealous of him, as is always the case among children in a family. However, his sisters also loved him and did many things for him. They washed his laundry and cleaned his bedroom. His mother loved to see her daughters assisting their brother. She may have thought that the help the girls gave to their brother was good training for them. Later they would have to care for their husbands and families.

As a child Sangaya had no toys manufactured in a factory. He made his own toys as many African children do, even to this day. He made toys from clay, wood, grass and other readily available materials. Sangaya made miniature cows, goats, people and huts. In the new changing Malawi, cars, watches, guitars and gramophones were brought into the country, and the young Sangaya grew familiar with these foreign things, too. His curiosity was kindled by these new inventions. The result was that Sangaya's collection of toys included little guitars, cars, cows, huts, etc.

His School Days

In 1913 Sangaya went to school at the HHI Primary School. At that time the headmaster was George Hall, a missionary from Scotland. Sangaya enjoyed learning new things. His school subjects were arithmetic, geography, English language and music. While at school, Sangaya bought himself a guitar, which enabled him to form a band. This band was made up of four school-boys who played for wedding parties and won itself a name in Blantyre.

From 1914 to 1918 education in Malawi was disrupted. The First World War took many teachers away from their work. HHI Primary School was not an exception. Out of the ten teachers, six were conscripted to serve in the army, and only four teachers remained. This situation almost caused the school to close down. However, it survived the wartime, and Sangaya was able to continue with his education. In 1924 he was one of the few boys who passed the old Standard Six examination with flying colours. At that time Standard Six was the highest level of education one could achieve. Therefore, Sangaya had acquired the highest level of mission education available in the land. It is true that the education standard set then was much higher than that of today. It is not surprising that, with that education, Sangaya later became General Secretary of the Synod of Blantyre. He continued to be an effective leader well into the late 1970s, when highly educated young clergy were on the increase in the ranks of the church.

From 1924 to 1926, Sangaya trained as a teacher at the Henry Henderson Institute at Blantyre Mission. The training was for two years. In mid 1926 he graduated as an English Grade Teacher. This was a special certificate which qualified him to teach senior classes. Formerly this position had been reserved for Europeans only.

His Marriage

Jonathan met Christian Mtingala at the Henry Henderson Institute in 1926. At that time Jonathan was in his final year of training as a teacher. At that time HHI was both a training school for teachers and a Primary School. The Primary School was divided into two separate sections, one for boys and one for girls. Christian was in the primary school for girls as a pupil doing her Standard Three.

After Jonathan completed his training as a teacher, he was posted to Malabvi Primary School. On weekends Jonathan would go to the HHI Girls School to visit Christian. It was not easy for girls in the boarding school to meet with boys even on weekends. Staying in a boarding school, as Christian did, meant that her movements were restricted. Christian recalls that Mrs E. Benzies, the boarding school mistress at the girls' school, was very strict with girls. She did not allow them to go out of school bounds and neither did she allow boys to come to see the girls in the school. To overcome this problem, sometimes the boys came with made-up messages of an emergency nature for particular girls in order to have them released. Jonathan successfully tried this method for getting Christian out of the brick walls where the girls were confined.

At the end of 1926, Christian completed the Standard Three and decided to leave school at that time. She taught at Makata Primary School in 1927 as an unqualified pupil teacher. There it was easy for her to meet often with Jonathan. Jonathan and Christian's friendship and courtship lasted for three years, enabling the two young people to get to know each other well. In 1929, Jonathan and Christian were married in St Michael and All Angels Church at the Blantyre Mission. The officiating clergyman was Rev. Henry Kambwiri Matecheta, one of the first ordained Malawians in the Blantyre Synod, ordained with two others in 1911.

Christian says she wore a white dress and white shoes at the wedding. These articles were bought specially for the wedding by Jonathan. Customarily a young man was expected to buy his bride a new dress for her to wear on the wedding day. Previously the colour of the dress did not matter, but with the coming of missionaries who introduced a new way of life, white became the accepted colour for brides. Jonathan himself wore a grey suit and black shoes. The wedding cake, another new thing in African weddings, was baked by Mrs Hanna Mlanga. The reception was held at Ndirande near Chinseu market.

Jonathan and Christian made their home at Ndirande near the Mlanga and Bismarck families. From there, Jonathan walked to work at HHI Primary School every day. Jonathan was transferred from Malabvi back to HHI in 1928. This is why he was residing at Ndirande after the wedding. Except for domestic servants, Africans were not allowed to reside on the Mission Station in those days.

His Wife, Christian

Christian had a noble background. Her father, Robin Mtingala, a teacher and evangelist at Namaka Primary School, was a brother of Chief Chitela I, and Chief Mpama I of Chiradzulu District. In her up-bringing, Christian moved among the royalty of her family and mixed well with people from many backgrounds.

Materially, Christian was well provided for, and her parents were liberal in dealing with her. When many parents in the 1920s were reluctant to send their daughters to school, Christian's parents put her in a school near her home. There she did so well that she had to be sent to HHI where she attained Standard Three, a rare achievement for girls at that time. Christian had a strong background and adequate education, which later strengthened her role as a leader of the Mvano (the women's organisation of Blantyre Synod) and as wife of the General Secretary.

This is the translation from Chichewa of a letter to Christian in her role as the chairperson of the Mvano (translation by Farai Ncozana):

Mission Mulanje
Mulanje

5-1-69

The Chairperson of Blantyre
Women's Guild

Dear Mrs Sangaya

Thank you very much for the donation of 20 shillings towards help-ing orphans. Please pass on our gratitude to the members of the women's guild for their donation and that we will always remember them.

Now we have two children, a baby girl who is ten months old and a four days old baby boy. Before this infant, we had another child of 18 months old who has gone home. Unfortunately, that child is unable to hold its head in place. As the mother is no longer at the hospital but in the village, she is unable to give proper care to the child.

In 1968, we had 1892 new born babies. This large number was more than the past years.

We are very happy that we are receiving many women who are coming to the hospital for help. Still, there are some women who do not come for help. Last month three women were brought from the village with ruptured uteruses. They were very sick but they survived.

Greeting to the members of the Women's Guild and thank you very much.

From

Dr R.G. Dabb

When the Sangaya family moved to Blantyre Mission in 1954, Mrs Sangaya showed interest in Mvano. She interested younger women in joining the organisation, and consequently, young women such as E. Chisanga, M. Bis-marck and others joined Mvano and later became leaders of the organisation. From Blantyre, Mrs Sangaya was able to visit Mvano groups in Nsanje, Chi-kwawa, Mwanza, Mulanje, Zomba and many other places within the Synod of Blantyre. In her travels, Mrs Sangaya led Bible Study Meetings and taught the women about the importance of their involvement in the life and work of the church.

Outside the Synod of Blantyre, Mrs Sangaya participated in many women's meetings. In 1958, she attended a meeting in Lilongwe organised by the Christian Council. She was the chairperson of that conference and played a significant role in uniting women from various denominations.

Mrs Sangaya loved to work with children. At Blantyre Mission, she taught Sunday School for many years. There she enjoyed teaching children Bible stories, following the Christian Year Calendar. One of the best times of the year for her was harvest time. She explained:

> Ndimakonda kwambiri ikafika nthawi ya masika chifukwa inali nthawi yoti ana onse amayamika Mulungu pamodzi ndi aphunzitsi awo. Ana onse amatenga chimanga chimodzi kapena mazira. Akatero ndiye onse amaima pa mzere ali yense atanyamula mphatso yake. Ine ndiye ndimayenda patsogolo tili kuchokera ku kalasi kumapita kukalowa mutchalitchi. Potuluka tinkachita chimodzimodzi.

> (The translation reads:) I was always very happy when harvest time came, because it was a time when all the Sunday School children, together with their teachers, went into the church to praise God. Every child brought a cob of maize or some eggs. They would all line up, carrying their gifts. I would walk in front of them, coming from the Sunday School classroom going into the church. We would then leave the church in the same way as we had entered.

Their Children

Jonathan and Christian were blessed with seven children, three sons and four daughters. Two of them died; a boy named John died at the age of 25 in 1971, and a girl named Gertrude died in 1949 at the age of two.

Of their surviving children, McNeil (who died in 1996) was the first born. His likeness to his father was such that when he grew up, he was always mistaken for his father. He took the stature of his father, suffered the same eye disease (high blood pressure of the eye) as his father, and like his father wore spectacles. Like his father, McNeil also served in the Army as an E2 and intelligence officer. He rose to the same rank, Warrant Officer, Class 2, that his father obtained. He would also have been a minister of religion, like his father, had he felt the call. But when Rev. S. Green invited McNeil to join the ministry after his 10 years of service in the Army, he felt happy to remain a "Senior Christian", i.e. a respectable Christian who had served the church a long time without necessarily holding an official position. Green was a pastor at St Michael and All Angels Church when Sangaya was ordained in 1952, after his training. In 1955, McNeil joined the Civil Service as a clerk and retired in 1974, having served as Head Clerk, District Commissioner, Senior Commissioner and Chief Traditional Courts Commissioner.

Alexander was the second born son. He was born in 1932. When he grew up, he married and worked in many capacities, including plant operator, carpenter, machine operator and lorry driver. He retired in 1979, having faithfully served the Malawi Government for many years, and died in 1998.

Fanny was the third born. After her education she worked as a primary school teacher. She then was married to John Matenje, the General Manager of the Christian Literature Association in Malawi. Today she runs a small restaurant business in Lunzu.

From left to right: Eleanor, Mrs Sangaya, Rev. J.D. Sangaya, John, McNeil, Merium (granddaughter), Hilda (granddaughter) and Douglas (grandson). At Chileka Airport travelling to Scotland, 1961.

Lilian was the fourth born. She worked for Hetherwick Press as a Manageress in the binding section. She was married to Mr Nyundo, and later was divorced. She continued to work for Hetherwick Press until she died in 1997.

The fifth born, Eleanor, trained as teacher. She also studied home economics in Australia. She was married to Y. Mkandawire and had two children. They were later divorced. For about 10 years she stayed at Namaka doing farming alongside her mother. She then was married to Mr Kanyuka. Later she rejoined the Ministry of Education and was promoted to the position of District Education Officer.

It is obvious that Sangaya's children were brought up well, and became useful citizens. Their contributions, in their various fields of work, added in modest ways to the development of Malawi. It may also be of interest to note that from these five children, Sangaya was the proud grandfather of 23 grandchildren.

The Teacher

In 1927, Sangaya taught Junior Primary School at Malabvi. His one year there convinced his superiors that he was an able teacher with a lot of potential. In 1928, he was transferred to HHI Senior Primary School at Blantyre Mission. Still demonstrating his capabilities, Sangaya was elevated to school supervisor in 1930. This post is equivalent to that of school inspector today.

Attracted by the possibilities of earning more money in the copper mines of Zambia, Sangaya deserted his work at Blantyre Mission in 1932 and set off on foot for Zambia. We do not know where he stayed in Zambia, but he was there for only two months. He was brought back to Blantyre Mission by one of the Blantyre missionaries who must have been in Zambia attending a church conference.

Back at Blantyre Mission, Sangaya was suspended as a lesson, to him and others, not to run away. For six months, he stayed quietly at his house at Ndirande. However, when he was reinstated, he was promoted to the position of head teacher and taught Standard Six, the final class in those days. He took over the head teachership from Cedrick Masangano, who retired in that year. It should be noted that the head teacher in those days was more in charge of his fellow teachers than being the general administrator of the school, a responsibility which was left in the hands of the headmaster. Today these two positions are merged into one.

Sangaya was revered and feared by students at the same time. They revered him because he was one of the first Malawians to be entrusted with the responsibility of teaching the highest class level, and at the same time he was to be one of the earliest African head teachers. He was feared because of his strictness. One of his former students, E. Zammimba, says this about him, "When he looked at you, it was as if you were faced by a bull ready to charge at you." It is true. Sangaya had an overpowering character which would make his students fear him. Yet the man was kind and generous.

His Retirement

After serving as a teacher for 22 years, Sangaya retired in January 1948 in order for him to join the ordained ministry. The Mission Council responsible for the running of missionary work, including Church schools, accepted Sangaya's retirement, but turned down his request for a pension. Previously, the Mission Council passed a resolution saying that people already working for the Church would no longer receive pension if they switched from one job to another within the establishment. Sangaya sought the support of Mr R. Paterson, Headmaster for Henry Henderson Institute.

> I beg to ask your support on the question of my services at HHI as a teacher for the past years. I have been a teacher at HH Institute for twenty-two years. My services terminated on 31st January this year (1948) so that I follow the call of our Lord Jesus Christ. Therefore, I take this opportunity to lodge in my petition through the Headmaster of the HHI to Mission Council. If I remained a teacher, there is no doubt, I would pension from the Mission Council and if I worked for the government during the past 22 years, I would be granted with a gratuity.

Mr Paterson presented the petition to the Mission Council, but without success. Unfortunately, Sangaya was the first victim of the Mission Council's ruling. Following his training for the ministry at Mulanje, Sangaya served the mission for 30 years, making a total of 52 years. As he died in active service, Sangaya did not retire and did not receive his pension. He blessed the Church with his unreserved services, as we shall see below.

22

Service in the Army

Sangaya's quest for adventure had not been suppressed by the punishment he had received from the missionaries at Blantyre Mission when he ran away to Zambia. In 1943, he joined the King's African Rifles. This was during the Second World War. He served in the army as an Education and Intelligence Officer. As a soldier, his active service was in East Africa and Madagascar. One informant says that Sangaya also went to the Far East, serving in Burma, India and Korea, but there is no clear evidence about this. Sangaya was demobilized in 1945 at the end of the war. By then he had risen to the rank of Warrant Officer, Class 2. This was the highest rank an African could achieve in the Army. After the war, Sangaya returned to HHI Primary School and took charge of the Junior Primary School until 1948. It was in 1947 that Sangaya decided to enter the ordained ministry of the CCAP Synod of Blantyre.

The Ordained Ministry

In 1948, Sangaya joined the theological college at Mulanje Mission. In his class there were seven students: M.G. Chikwesele, J.B. Lamya, C. Nkunga, S. Kaliati, D. Piringu, W. Pembereka, and S. Mleule. The course was for three years. Their tutors were the Revs S. Green and Charles Watt, the principal, Scottish missionaries whose scholarship was well matched by their smart dressing and punctuality. Sangaya strove to emulate his great mentor, Charles Watt. He disciplined himself, organising his time of study, his time to be with his family and his leisure time. It is not surprising that Sangaya graduated at the top of his class in almost every subject. The subjects he studied included: Church History, Old Testament studies, New Testament studies, Homiletics, Church Government, Greek and Latin. In spite of his position in class, Sangaya humbled himself before his fellow students. One of his classmates at the time, Rev. Cedric Nkunga, has this to say about him: "We knew that Jonathan would be our leader and a great leader in our church. He often walked behind us carrying our briefcases."

John McCracken has argued that the participation of Africans in the First and Second World Wars removed the myth held by both Whites and Africans that Whites were a superior race, and were the custodians of peace, freedom and progress. Many African soldiers, including Sangaya, who returned home after the war had seen the arrogance of whites, and were hardened by the experience. We do not have Sangaya's own reasons for deciding to join the ordained ministry. However, three points seem to have led him to his decision.

First, Sangaya had grown up with the mission. As a young boy he had gone to Sunday School, attended church services, and had seen missionary ministers and a few of his own fellow African ministers active in the ministry. He saw ministry being done, and with his own adventurous spirit, may have thought that he too could do it.

Second, during the war Sangaya may have seen some of the white men brutally killing each other. They had previously taught Sangaya about the love of God, the need to be at peace with every race or ethnic group and what it meant to be civilized. Sangaya may have been disappointed by the whites' failure to abide by the Gospel of love and peace they had always preached. He, on the other hand, was determined to preach and put the Gospel into practice.

Third, and not least, Sangaya may have been fully convinced in his heart that God himself was calling him to be his servant - full-time. As a teacher, deacon and elder in those days, Sangaya had ample opportunity for preaching the Word of God, but that was not enough. Now he wanted to be engaged as a full-time pastor. The urge for more money, evident in his earlier years, had vanished, and the only way left for him was total commitment to God. Indeed Sangaya became a great leader in the CCAP, as well shall see later. Here it is enough to say that he graduated with a Certificate in Theology and was ordained in 1952.

In his active ministry, Sangaya first served in Ntcheu at Bemvu as an Assistant Minister under Rev. Harry Matecheta. The area he served stretched from Ntcheu to Matope. In 1954 he was transferred to Blantyre Mission where he served as an Associate Minister at St Michael and All Angels. The Senior Minister then was Rev. Alistair Rennie. It was there that he met the Queen Mother when she visited Malawi in 1957.

As a pastor, Sangaya enjoyed visiting his parishioners, encouraging them in their faith. He organized and ran training courses for his elders and church choir groups. He liked children and always met with them and taught Bible stories in Sunday School. He worked untiringly in evangelizing his area of ministry in Blantyre.

In 1961, Sangaya was appointed Assistant General Secretary. Then the General Secretary was Rev. Andrew Doig. Sangaya, being a good student all his life, quickly caught up with office management, dealing with personnel matters and getting to know the political and

The Queen Mother at St Michael and All Angels in Blantyre. From left to right: Rev. A. Rennie, Mrs Rennie, J.D. Sungaya and Rev. H.K. Matecheta.

civil leaders. Soon Rev. Doig saw in Sangaya an African church leader who could ably take over the leadership of the church from missionaries. He worked with Sangaya, preparing him to be General Secretary.

General Secretary

In 1961, Sangaya went to Scotland where he studied church administration for one year. When he returned home in 1962, he took over the General Secretaryship from Rev. Doig. The latter assumed the position of Assistant General Secretary. This exchange of positions was a sign that the Synod of Blantyre was becoming truly indigenous. Sangaya became the first Malawian General Secretary of the Synod of Blantyre, a position he held with dignity until his death.

The unique position occupied by Sangaya as the first African General Secretary began without any ceremony to talk about. The Mission Council was composed of missionaries only. They were formerly responsible for planning missionary activities and recruitment of staff. They recommended Sangaya's name to the Blantyre Synod meeting. As was the case with all recommendations which emanated from the Mission Council, the Synod accepted them without question. Because the Council members were the leaders of the missionary church, Sangaya's name was accepted without question.

When one considers that missionaries were viewed by Malawians at that time as the messengers of a new religion, a new way of life, prophets of truth and distributors of material benefits, for Sangaya to have been appointed to succeed a missionary church leader, was to be highly privileged. He was seen by many people in church circles, as well as outside, as having assumed the authority formerly vested in missionaries. Sangaya himself may have been convinced that, at least in the initial years of his leadership, he was an embodiment of missionaries. Therefore, it is not surprising that Sangaya became a father figure, whose authority was recognised by all. As one missionary commented, "Sangaya seemed to me to be a traditional chief in Blantyre, hearing carefully, observing, then making decisions."

There is no doubt that Sangaya was a good listener and was also quick in understanding issues presented to him. Rev. Doig, who worked closely with Sangaya, said about him,

> I used to marvel as I handed over to him issues of land, property and finance, how quickly he grasped the essentials and made decisions without fuss. He never allowed administrative responsibilities to detract him from pastoral and preaching work. He travelled freely and effectively in the presbyteries and parishes.

Sangaya was a rare combination of an administrator and pastor whose influence touched all the sections of society. Jean Watt said about him, "Although he often moved with the highest of the land, he never forgot his basic calling as a minister of the faithful and as a preacher of the Gospel."

Sangaya also loved the best of the past, too, and would preserve the wise and authentically sound traditions of old. For example, he strongly believed that young people must always respect older people in accordance with Malawian culture. However, Sangaya also would have the young respected for the new knowledge they had acquired through education.

During this period, the old building of St Michael and All Angels Church developed structural weaknesses which endangered the building. Sangaya drew on all the resources he could in Malawi and outside, in order to preserve the building. He said, "We cannot let this historical building fall when its care is in our hands. We must preserve it so that our great-grandchildren can enjoy the fruits of the past." The repair work included the complete rebuilding of the two inside pillars at the front of the church and the adding of reinforcement bars between the pillars. The repair work was completed in 1979, a few months before Sangaya died.

We could recount further examples and incidents to show that Sangaya's leadership in the life and work of the Synod of Blantyre was indeed felt in every corner of it. Here it is enough to say that his dedication was resolute. This became faithfully apparent after his death. Sangaya did not spare himself whenever there was something to be done. This writer remembers many times when Sangaya denied himself food and drink to put right a problem facing the Synod.

We have noted that Sangaya's leadership in the life and work of the Synod of Blantyre was distinctive. He was a bridge between the mission church and the indigenous church. "He had a large mind and heart and a capacity to care for all." Sangaya accepted change when it was good and necessary for the church or for the welfare of God's children. He struggled for change and worked for it "with the enthusiasm of a new convert". This was because he loved God. His faith in him never faltered even when faced with apparently insurmountable obstacles. "His was a faith that truly moved many mountains and flung them into the sea."

Sangaya was well respected among politicians. His advice and counsel was always sought. For many years he was chaplain to the Mayor of the City of Blantyre. It was also often said of him that he was an advisor of Dr H. Kamuzu Banda, then Life President of the Republic of Malawi. Sangaya was often invited to the Palace to meet with local, state and international leaders.

However, Sangaya readily sacrificed his friendship and popularity with those in political power whenever there was need to do so. For example, in 1978, Sangaya went to attend an All Africa Council of Churches meeting in Zambia. While he was there, he met with Willie Chokani, Harry Bwanausi and others who were Dr Banda's political opponents, and had run away from Malawi in 1964 for fear of their lives. When Sangaya

returned to Malawi after the one week conference in Lusaka, he was inter-
rogated by the Malawi Police. When he admitted that he had indeed met
the dissidents in Zambia, Sangaya was driven to Zomba, where he was
kept by the police for three days. Asked why he had met in Zambia the
men who had rebelled against the "Ngwazi", Sangaya replied, "I am not a
politician but a religious leader. As a religious leader, I minister to both
bad and good, to both high and low." Here Sangaya communicated his
unbreakable leadership and total obedience to his Lord. He was not prepared to compromise his faith and leadership for cheap popularity. There is
no doubt that Sangaya was not a carbon copy of missionaries. While he
preserved some good missionary ways of doing church business, he also
initiated new ways and asserted his individuality.

Sangaya and the Winds of Change

Sangaya's social responsibility was moulded by two periods that he lived
in, the imperial or colonial era and the independence era. The imperial era
in Malawi began in 1898 when Scottish missionaries invited the British
Crown to protect the country from the Portuguese in Mozambique. This
was because the Portuguese threatened to annex Malawi to Mozambique.
So, the British Crown sent Sir Harry Johnson to establish a protectorate
under it. To enforce the new political administration, traders and settlers
from Britain also came. Unlike the missionaries who came before them and
were close to the indigenous people, the newcomers looked down upon the
local people. Malawians, especially those educated in mission schools,
observed that the newcomers grabbed land and political power from the
owners of the land. Consequently, civil debating clubs began among educated Malawians. Many missionaries supported these debating clubs.
Popular topics often debated, according to Blantyre and Livingstonia
Synod records, included religion, education, agriculture, social development, and politics. The British traders and settlers in Malawi felt that missionaries spoiled Africans by giving them good education and treating them
as equals. For the newcomers, highly educated Africans grew such big
heads that they forgot that they were from a lower human breed than
Europeans. To safeguard their privileged position, the newcomers pre-
ferred a low education for Africans as this would retain the servant/master
relationship between the two races. This tension was a complete change
from the trust that had grown between missionaries and local people. Dur-

ing Sangaya's boyhood from 1910 to 1920 bitter feelings against white settlers grew strong among some local people. John Chilembwe's leading of a rebellion in Chiradzulu district is a case in point. Sangaya would not have been spared from the attitudes of that period. In spite of this, he was not prejudiced against whites in general.

The questions raised by Malawians against the British migrants in Malawi were acerbated by the two world wars. Malawians participated in both wars fighting on the British side. The survival instinct in the battle field knitted together blacks and whites. Sangaya was a soldier in the Second World War. His responsibility as Intelligence and Education officer in the army meant that he taught both blacks and whites. In times of peace, Sangaya would not, at that period, have taught whites due to the racial discrimination that prevailed. So, this was a change in Sangaya's consciousness. It gave him a new experience and self confidence. Though Malawian soldiers were treated fairly during the war, they did not know why they were fighting, especially when missionaries had preached against war. After the war in 1945, the fellowship that had bridged the gap between whites and blacks fell apart. It is not surprising that the Nyasaland African Congress was formed soon after that war. Levi Mumba, a former Livingstonia teacher then working for the government, was its secretary. Local people who returned from the war rejected the imperial authority and racial discrimination practised by white settlers. We have already noted that Sangaya was a soldier during that time. He joined the rejectionist approach of Malawians who suspected white settlers and the colonial government. At the height of African nationalism, the rejectionist approach developed into a "revolutionary tradition". This tradition was rooted in the idea of independence. India epitomised that independence when it got its freedom from the British during that period. Malawians grew confident in themselves. They rejected white settlers who grabbed their lands, they rejected British rule and they rejected being treated as second class citizens in their own land. How would Sangaya, who rubbed shoulders with ex-combatants turned politicians, escape the seeds of revolution in him? His friend, Rev. Tom Colvin was a revolutionary type, as noted already, and that is why the colonial government deported him from Malawi in 1958. So, Sangaya's first politics were civil. Later he changed to *the revolutionary tradition* that swept across Africa in the 1950s. As an ordained minister of religion, Sangaya was now comfortable among African nationalist leaders who agitated for independence. Some people knew him as a school master, others knew him as a soldier while others saw him as a pastor. Sangaya had participated in the Second World War and lived through the transition from colonial rule to independence.

When Malawi became independent in 1964, Sangaya was already General Secretary for the Synod of Blantyre. He was in the forefront of the service of worship at Kamuzu Stadium that marked the first independence celebrations. The new government invited Sangaya to the opening of Parliament and to many functions. As already noted, he was chaplain to the Mayor of the city of Blantyre. Sangaya was recognised and respected by those he had been with in the army and by those who simply knew him as their pastor or General Secretary. He adopted the new system of government, working to promote its vision of a new Malawi led by Africans. Therefore, his approach to socio-political concerns changed to *the adoptionist tradition.*

Following the *Cabinet crisis* of 1964, a few months after independence, many political leaders whom Sangaya knew personally fled the country for fear of their lives. The new Malawi government expelled missionaries who sided with the dissidents. Andrew Ross, a missionary expelled by the same government, was Sangaya's friend. Further, Sangaya knew many families who lost their loved ones through torture and MCP brutality. As we have already noted, Sangaya experienced first hand MCP government harassment when police arrested him on his return from Zambia. The hope that Sangaya had in the new Malawi and its government was shattered. So, Sangaya's socio-political concerns changed to *the tradition of silence.* The basis for this approach is fear and the instinct for survival. Sangaya did not want to go back to the trenches of 1943 but he was disappointed with the new order. Sangaya wanted peace because he saw first hand the ugliness of war. Now, his main concern was to uplift the spiritual well being of the new nation of Malawi and his position as the first Malawian General Secretary gave power to do so. Though Sangaya stood his ground when it was necessary to do so, he did it alone like a prophet. He carried the burden alone without involving the Church that he led. In spite of this, Sangaya successfully withstood the winds of change.

His Vision of the Church in Malawi

Sangaya viewed the church as essentially relevant to the whole of life, giving it character, integrity and hope. For him, the proclamation of the Gospel was complete only if it was matched by an equal emphasis on service. He envisioned the church as the body of Christ composed of men and women, young and old, with all taking their part in it. It is not surprising that Sangaya served in numerous secular and religious committees. These committee included: Playgroup Association of Malawi, Hogg Robinson Insurance Company, Blantyre Water Board, HHI Secondary School Board, Private Hospital Association of Malawi, Christian Service Committee, Christian Council, Religious Broadcast Advisory Board and others. In each of these committees and boards, Sangaya aimed at sharing Jesus Christ and His call for everyone to be disciples and for the church to be salt in the world.

Further, Sangaya's vision of the church was that of a growing church, able to govern itself, financially support itself, and capable of being responsible for propagating the Gospel. In order to achieve this vision, Sangaya introduced intensive leadership training programmes at Chilema Lay Training Centre, Chigodi Women's Centre and Likhubula Youth Centre. Through these training programmes able leaders emerged who were capable of enabling the church to become truly indigenous and autonomous. Sangaya yearned to see "a church alive for Christ and expressing its love for him in generous financial provision for His church that it might serve in fullness and freedom."

While Sangaya rejoiced in the special place of the CCAP within the country and outside it, he desired close links with other churches in every possible joint action. Tom Colvin remembers, "He treasured the historic links with the Church of Scotland. He never was tired of speaking about all he gained from his time in Scotland."

From the point of view of ecumenism and church unity, Sangaya saw denominationalism as a setback to the spreading of the Gospel and the growth of the church. His dream was to see an African church under African leadership. To this end, he worked with leaders of various churches including Anglican, Roman Catholic, Providence Industrial Mission, Zambezi Mission and so forth. In the Christian Council of Malawi, Sangaya was actively involved in church unity. The result of his efforts was that understanding was fostered among churches which previously did not see eye to eye. Sangaya was instrumental in the establishing of a joint CCAP and Anglican Lay Training Centre at Chilema in 1967. He joined hands with Bishop Donald Arden in building the centre as well as staffing it. Over 4,000 men, women and youth were to be involved in Chilema projects each year, learning together, as disciples of Christ, about their unity in Christ.

In 1976, Nkhoma Theological College was under heavy attack from the Malawi Congress Party (MCP) Regional Office in Lilongwe. Rev. Stephen Kauta Msiska, the Principal of Nkhoma Theological College at that time, taught students in a homiletics class that it was improper for a preacher to wear Dr Banda's badge, a sign of loyalty to the Life President, Ngwazi Kamuzu Banda, and the MCP, while in the pulpit, as this would detract the attention of listeners in the congregation. On theological grounds, according to Kauta, the wearing of the head of state badge by a preacher in the pulpit was in conflict with the preacher's allegiance to Christ, whom he should hold supreme and above all earthly rulers. It was more true at that time, when people were forced to wear the badge, than it is now that the demands of the head of state were in direct competition with the demands of the Gospel of Jesus Christ.

To continue the story, it was one of the Nkhoma Synod students who reported to the MCP that Kauta was preventing theological students from wearing Dr Banda's badge. In the MCP view, Kauta was subversive and disrespectful of the State President. From the Regional Office of the MCP in Lilongwe to Nkhoma came Mr J.T. Kumbweza, the Regional Minister. When he threatened all the students and lecturers at Nkhoma, it was Sangaya who saved the situation. When Kumbweza addressed the students and staff demanding an explanation, Sangaya stood up. Using African wisdom he said, "When a big man, an old or important man, has spoken, no young ones are allowed to speak". He then ordered the students and staff to stand up while he ushered the Regional Minister out of the room. That was at the end of a day, which without Sangaya being present, might have ended with arrests or worse, in bloodshed. Of course, the College was closed soon after this incident and Rev. S. Kauta lost his job and was sent to his village unceremoniously. A fresh start in a new place was necessary for the College.

Sangaya was at the forefront of moving the CCAP Theological College from Nkhoma to Blantyre and later to Zomba where it would be close to the University of Malawi. He also wanted to see this College opening its doors to other denominations. Consequently, the Anglican Church began to send its candidates for theological training first to Nkhoma and then to Zomba in 1978.

Later the Anglican Church became a full member of the theological board of the college. Another ecumenical enterprise which Sangaya undertook was the formation of the Christian Service Committee (CSC) of the Churches in Malawi, and the Private Hospital Association of Malawi (now known as CHAM). As Tom Colvin put it, "I can say without hesitation that if it had not been for his (Sangaya's) enthusiasm and encouragement in the early days, there would have been no Christian Service Committee and no Private Hospital Association in Malawi today." The Christian Service Committee began as the service arm of Blantyre Synod, under the direction of Sangaya as General Secretary of the Synod in 1965. At that time it was called the Utumiki Project. In 1967 the MCP government closed it down on suspicion that it could have been a subversive agent. This suspicion arose out of its massive response in aiding Mozambican refugees in Mangochi District. In 1968 it restarted under a new name, the Christian Service Committee. Later as the service arm of the Christian Council. When this service arm of the Synod expanded, Sangaya invited the Rev. P. Mzembe of

The Christian Service Committee of the Churches of Malawi. From left to right: Fr Michael Levaast, Bishop Donald Arden, Mrs Barbara Rodgers, Archbishop Chiona, Dr. H. Kamuzu Banda, Rev. J.D. Sangaya, Bishop L.P. Hardman, Fr. Adrian van der Hulst, Fr. G. van der Asdonk, Andrew Kishindo, S. Grant, Chief Mbelwa III.

Livingstonia Synod, who had expressed doubts, and the Rev. K. Mgawi of Nkhoma Synod, to join them in this new way of working together. In the formation of the CHAM, and the CSC, Sangaya was in the forefront, encouraging church leaders to try this new way of cooperating in medical and social services.

In the All African Conference of Churches (AACC), Sangaya was a celebrated figure. Rev. George Mambo, then coordinator of the AACC's Development Desk, said about him, "The old man [Sangaya] was one of the strong pillars of the church in Africa. His participation in the AACC's Executive Committee and other committees of the AACC was significant. We loved him for his sense of humour and his wisdom". Through his efforts to link the Synod of Blantyre with other churches in Africa, Sangaya encouraged Malawian church leaders to travel to various countries within Africa. They learned, first-hand, new ways which Christians in those lands had developed to meet the demands of the Gospel in their situations.

His Farm

In 1969 Sangaya attempted to purchase from the government 35 acres of land near Njuli. This is on the Blantyre/Zomba road. He intended to settle there. As village people had already encroached the parcel of land, the negotiations between Sangaya and government failed. Sangaya did not give up. He approached Mr Frank Scott whose farm was near Namaka market with a view to buying some land from him. Scott agreed to sell 50 acres to Sangaya. By the end of the same year (1969) the two people finalised the deal. Early in 1970 Sangaya was a proud owner of a fifty acre farm where he planted maize and other crops. He also had a few dairy cattle and sheep. Mrs Sangaya moved in 1971 from Blantyre mission to settle and manage their new home and farm located close to Namaka market. This is only six kilometres north east of Njuli, where Sangaya originally tried to purchase land. So, he was satisfied with his new home. Sangaya first built a house out of sun dried bricks. Later he built a permanent red brick house that his widow still occupies. All his time, Sangaya stayed at Blantyre Mission and only went to stay with his wife at the farm when he was free from Synod duties. He never allowed his personal projects and life to sway him away from his responsibility as the servant of God and General Secretary for the Synod of Blantyre.

His Influence on the Life and Work of the Synod

"It could be said that as General Secretary of Blantyre Synod, Sangaya was the embodiment of the 'take-over' and of the integration of mission and church." In the take-over that Tom Colvin speaks of, Scottish missionaries handed over the power and the administration of the church to Africans. The task of establishing an authentic African church and the integrating of that church with the mission was all invested in the leadership of Sangaya. Being the first Malawian General Secretary of the Synod of Blantyre, Sangaya served as a test case of the Africans' ability to lead the church into the future. In the past, all leadership positions in the church were held by missionaries as already noted. It is also true that Sangaya's success or failure in the "take-over" would provide evidence of how well the missionaries had trained Africans to take top leadership positions in the church. Therefore, the success of an indigenous church depended on how well Sangaya exercised his leadership and on how well the missionaries and the whole church supported him.

The immediate problem that Sangaya faced in his administration was the acute shortage of ordained Malawian ministers. First, the ones ordained in 1911 and 1914 were too old to work effectively and were dying one by one due to old age. By the end of 1962, the year Sangaya took office, the only remaining elderly Malawian minister, Rev. Matecheta, died. This left Sangaya without older African leadership to whom he could turn for help in matters concerning the past.

Second, the problem of shortage of personnel was exacerbated by the fact that long serving missionaries having handed over the church and leadership to the indigenous people, were returning to Scotland for good. The funds that previously came from Scotland to Malawi in support of missionary activities were greatly reduced, since the church was now under local leadership. The legacy of huge mission stations built by missionaries, now left without funds for maintenance, was a financial burden on the young leadership. At the same time, fewer hands were available to carry on with the growing church work.

On the other hand, the above problems, seen from a different angle, were a blessing to Sangaya's leadership. That the original core of local leadership had all died meant that there was no one who would cling to the idea that, "this is the way things were done by missionaries, and they should remain that way". In the same way, the exodus of missionaries and the reduction of funds to support the work of the church gave room for new initiatives by the now indigenous church led by Sangaya.

Therefore, Sangaya, as General Secretary, had open opportunity to introduce changes without necessarily having to refer to either African leaders or missionaries who preceded him. His workmates all over the Synod of Blantyre, both Malawian and European, were younger and closer to Sangaya in thinking and outlook on church life than the generation we have noted above.

In order to deal with the acute shortage of ordained ministers, in 1963 Sangaya joined hands with Rev. P.C. Mzembe, the General Secretary of Livingstonia Synod, and Rev. K. Mgawi, the General Secretary of Nkhoma Synod. The three General Secretaries agreed to establish a joint theological college at Nkhoma, replacing the three small colleges which each Synod operated separately. The college at Nkhoma was headed by Rev. Charles Watt, a distinguished theologian and scholar from Edinburgh. The Faculty included J. Mwale, C. Chinkhadze, J. Steytler, S. Faiti and S. Kauta, who later succeeded Watt as Principal.

Sangaya's idea of a joint theological college was advantageous to the three Synods in a number of ways. First, it was financially cheaper for the Synods to work cooperatively than for each Synod to have its own college. In the joint operation of the college, the three Synods pooled together theological lecturers, and used the same facilities such as buildings, libraries and so forth. Second, the number of students was increased in the joint college, and the quality of theological training was improved. For example, qualification for entry into the college was raised from Primary School Leaving Certificate to MSCE, i.e., four years of secondary school education. At the same time, the curriculum in the college was improved to suit the local situation. African Réligions, previously not included in the curriculum, was introduced as a subject to be taught. This assisted the new leadership to sharpen the African perspective in theological education and in church life. The result of this joint college, with its stress on high academic standards and contexualization of theology was that:

- leaders who emerged out of the college were able to define their faith intelligently and reflectively, using African idioms and thought forms in their relating to and understanding of the Gospel.

- the new leaders were united by living and learning together, a sure way of unifying the church and fostering a strong Christian community throughout Malawi.

- church leaders, in keeping with the new nation of Malawi where young men and women acquired high education, were taking leadership positions in government as well as in industry. Some of these young people were adventurous and wanted to exert their Africanness in many ways, including in worship. With the new trained leadership, the church was able to provide some direction in this self-examination and self-understanding.

In 1978, the joint theological college at Nkhoma was closed down as we noted already. When it reopened, Sangaya moved it to Blantyre and then to Zomba, near the University of Malawi. Sangaya's reason for moving the college near the University was obvious. He wanted theological students to have access to the University Library and to challenge them to aspire for a University education. Even though Sangaya did not live to see his dream come true, today many ordained ministers hold Malawi University degrees, and are knowledgeable leaders in a truly African church.

In 1977 there was a financial crisis in the Synod of Blantyre. Several factors caused the crisis. First, the number of ordained ministers increased, but was not accounted for when the budget for that year was drawn. So this inflated expenditure tilted the balance sheet. Second, due to the rise in the cost of living, ministers demanded a one hundred percent stipend increase. When Sangaya asked the meeting where the extra money to pay them would come from, some clerics argued, *"Chikhulupiriro chanu chiri kuti?* Where is your faith?"* Using the Bible to respond to their argument, Sangaya quoted Matthew chapter 4 verses 5 and 6:

> Then the devil took him to the holy city and had him stand on the highest point of the temple. "If you are the Son of God," he said, "throw yourself down. For it is written:
>
> > "'He will command his angels concerning you,
> >   and they will lift you up in their hands,
> >   so that you will not strike your foot against a stone.'"

Through the two scriptures verses, Sangaya tried to show his colleagues that faith in God relates to the reality of his Kingdom. It cannot be equated with tangible *tambalas* and *kwachas*. The ministers ignored his wisdom. Their demand for more stipends was so strong that nothing would move them. Sangaya was convinced that the faith that his colleagues had would not increase the Synod's income by one hundred percent to meet their stipends. However, he proposed that meeting put one condition: that the one hundred percent increase of stipends would be on trial for three months. If the monthly Synod's income fail to march the expenditure, the stipends would revert to where they were before the meeting. This was agreed upon. Following that meeting, the ministers received their new stipends. Some Church programme expenses were cut to try balancing the accounts. In spite of this measure, the Synod ran at five thousand Kwacha deficit per month. The faith that the ministers spoke about did not work. So, Sangaya called representatives from all Presbyteries after the third month to review the situation. When he showed the figures at the meeting, no one argued to continue with the new stipend. Consequently, ministers' stipends were reduced by half, souring the relationship between them and the office staff including Sangaya. Some suspicious ministers went behind Sangaya's back to find out if his stipend and that of this writer had also been reduced. They found out that the two stipends had not been increased when the ministers demanded the one hundred percent increase. Apparently Sangaya's leadership was guided by good stewardship. He exercised what he believed and was pragmatic about financial matters.

The problem of diminishing support of church funds from Scotland, as we have already noted, faced Sangaya in his assumption of leadership. The new administration at first found it difficult to run the church with less funds. Soon it learned to do with the little money it received. More importantly, the new administration stressed good stewardship and taught congregations all over the Synod about the need to give generously to the church. Further, congregations learned to depend on themselves in putting up new churches and manses. The result was that self confidence was instilled in the minds of church members; they were proud to know that they owned the church buildings and that leadership was in their own hands. Due to the lasting foundation which Sangaya had built by cultivating good stewardship and a self-help spirit, today Blantyre Synod has developed its financial capacity so much that it is truly self-funding. It meets its recurrent budget and has investments in numerous buildings. The Synod has achieved all of these things because of the strong leadership foundation that was laid by Sangaya.

Another area in which Sangaya influenced the life of the Synod of Blantyre was by involvement of young people in the music of the church. In 1964, he interested secondary school students at HHI to form a choir group which would sing at St Michael and All Angels Church from time to time. (St Michael and All Angels is one of the most conservative congregations in the Synod of Blantyre; it is more Scottish in its worship than most congregations in Scotland.) Sangaya encouraged the choir to sing local tunes in that church. The choir was formed and led by Frighton Kuseka, who was a student at HHI, and was also a member of St. Michael's regular church choir, which was led by Mr E. Nkumba.

The church choir was different from the new secondary school choir in two ways. First, Nkumba's choir was made up of a mixed group of people taken from the congregation. The choir sang mostly Western tunes and was not flexible. The secondary school choir was homogeneous, i.e. was made up of students from one school, and the members were young boys and girls. The leader was himself a young person and a student. Therefore, when the new choir sang African tunes in St. Michael's Church, where the congregation was rigid in regard to the type of music in the order of worship, the choir was not welcome. Many elders criticized the choir as irresponsible and childish for bringing into the church tunes sung at beer parties in villages. Consequently, the choir was not allowed to sing in the church. Sangaya, who had encouraged the choir to form, did not lose heart because his idea of bringing some Africanness into the church through music was rejected. He encouraged the choir to sing at HHI Secondary School assembly every morning and promised to establish a Youth Department within the Synod. At the HHI school assembly, the choir was accepted and later became popular.

The new department which Sangaya promised to establish would be the instrument through which young people would participate in the life of the church and bring to it their new ideas, including the type of music Sangaya wanted introduced.

In 1965, Sangaya led a church delegation to Kampala in Uganda, where they attended the launching of the All Africa Conference of Churches.

Among the Malawi delegation was Mrs E. Makonyola, wife of one of the ministers of the Synod of Blantyre. Sangaya asked Mrs Makonyola to observe youth involvement in the assembly. Mrs Makonyola saw that there were young ordained ministers actively serving at the assembly. As this was her first time to see young ordained ministers, she was so impressed that when she returned to Malawi, her report about the assembly brought a strong recommendation to the Synod that young people must be involved in the life of the Synod to the extent of allowing their ordination as ministers. Sangaya saw this new idea blending well with his idea of introducing African tunes in the Synod through the involvement of young people.

Therefore, in 1967, Sangaya established a Youth Department within the Synod. Rev. G.C. Kayembe was appointed Youth Secretary and was directly responsible to the General Secretary. Later a Youth Committee was formed as a coordinating body and as an instrument for encouraging youth activities throughout the Synod. In 1968, this department was moved to Likhubula House in Mulanje, a very suitable place for outdoor activities for young people. Sangaya wanted to have young people on the Youth Committee, but this was not possible at that early stage because all the ministers were of mature age, and so were all the elders who sat in Synod committees. However, the new Youth Department soon influenced the whole Synod so much that by 1969 many young people had trained as Sunday School teachers, and a few had joined the Theological College to train for the ordained ministry. Many choir groups composed of young people had formed in many congregations throughout the Synod. They were singing African-composed hymns. It was during this period that the usage of drums in worship was also introduced in the church.

Sangaya believed in and loved youth work, as we have seen above. He personally worked regularly at Mpemba Boys' School, which is a reformatory school for delinquent children, located outside Blantyre on the road to Chikwawa. Sangaya devoted his time to going to this school whenever it was possible for him to do so. There he conducted Sunday worship and encouraged the boys to be responsible citizens. Sangaya took a special interest in working with children and young people, because he believed that this group was part of the church and therefore fundamental in the Africanization process of the church. Sangaya was satisfied when many young people were involved in the life of the church, including the ordained ministry.

Opening up the Synod of Blantyre to new partnerships was another contribution Sangaya made. During the missionary era, the Synod of Blantyre was a baby of the Church of Scotland. All its overseas personnel, funding, overseas visitors and material requirements came from Scotland. When the Synod sent students overseas for further training, they were sent to Scotland. Of course at that time, missionaries who were in Blantyre Synod all came from Scotland, and they did not look elsewhere for their needs and correspondence. They always corresponded with the home church.

However, when church leadership was handed over to the Malawians, the ties between Scotland and Blantyre Synod were loosened. In 1968, Sangaya found new partnerships, first with the Presbyterian Church in the United States (PCUSA). Some American missionaries were invited to Malawi to work for the Synod. For example, Dr Bruce Gannaway taught at Nkhoma Theological College, while other American missionaries worked for the Christian Service Committee. Funds for community development were sent to the CSC from the USA, and students from Malawi were invited to study in America. For example, Rev. N. Kapenda went to Virginia. Later, Sangaya also engaged the Presbyterian Church in Canada (PCC) in a partnership. In 1969, the PCC sent Rev. Brian Crosby to work in the Youth Department, which had been moved to Likhubula House as noted above.

Sangaya also made contacts with the Presbyterian Church in Ghana, and with the Presbyterian Church in East Africa (PCEA), with the same view of establishing partnerships. Rev. D.C. Sani was sent by the Synod of Blantyre to serve in the PCEA at St. Andrew's Church in Dar es Salaam. Sani served in Dar es Salaam for seven years before returning to Malawi in 1968. Sangaya's leadership had made this sharing of personnel possible by opening the Synod to new partnerships.

In order to strengthen the Synod's contacts and partnerships with other churches in Africa, Sangaya introduced the subject of partnership to the General Synod of the CCAP in 1969. It had been Sangaya's wish to have the General Synod of the CCAP join the AACC, but Nkhoma and Livingstonia Synods were reluctant to join this ecumenical organisation. Nkhoma Synod feared that the AACC might be a liberal organisation with communistic tendencies, which were contrary to its stance, so it would have nothing to do with that organisation. As for Livingstonia Synod, there was no real reason for its reluctance to join the AACC, except that the Livingstonia Synod feared that it might not fulfill its obligations, i.e. paying the required annual membership fee. In 1972, Sangaya had the Blantyre Synod, on its own, join the AACC. The other two Synods, to this day, have not joined the AACC. The Synod of Blantyre has continued with its membership in the AACC and benefited much from its link with this ecumenical family. Sangaya was happy to serve as a member of its Executive and General Committees in 1974-1978.

Travel was another way by which Sangaya influenced the life and work of Blantyre Synod. With the good partnerships he had established with churches overseas and in Africa, many visitors from these places came to visit the Synod of Blantyre. Conversely, the Synod, through Sangaya's leadership, sent many people to visit the various partner churches.

Here we will mention only a few individuals who travelled and found their experience enriching and rewarding for the whole church in Malawi. In 1968, Revs R. Masamba, S. Faiti and S. Chiphangwi went to Scotland for nine months. There they worked side by side with local ministers in city congregations in Edinburgh and Glasgow. This exposure widened the religious views of these ministers, and in turn they shared their own faith and perspectives about the church. When they returned to Malawi, their experience in Scotland came out clearly in the new positions they were assigned to by Sangaya. Rev. R. Masamba became the Deputy General Secretary of the Synod and Minister in charge of the St Michael and All Angels congregation. Rev. S. Faiti became a teacher in the Theological Education by Extension Programme in Malawi and later became its head. Rev. S. Chiphangwi served briefly at St Michael and All Angels Church as Assistant Minister, before being sent to Chancellor College of the University of Malawi to study for a BSocSc degree. Then Chancellor College was located at the present Chichiri Secondary School in Blantyre. Much later, he became a lecturer at Zomba Theological College, after which he became General Secretary of the Synod. These men and many others, men and women, who later travelled to other countries, were messengers of a mission church which had moved to be an indigenous church, or, indeed, just a church. Further, through these many travelled people, the Blantyre Synod was finding its rightful place as a church in Africa, and in the world.

Sangaya himself also travelled widely and left a lot of impressions in the minds of those he met. Several times he went to Scotland. In 1974, he went to Dumfries in Scotland and met a school teacher who still remembers him as "a very fine representative of his church." Sangaya had addressed children in a school in Dumfries, informing them about the Synod's involvement in education and evangelism. In 1977, Sangaya was invited to the United States of America by the Presbyterian Church there. In his visit he went to such places as New York, Indiana, Pittsburgh, Pennsylvania and Atlanta, Georgia. Sangaya's impact was felt by all who met him. For instance, at Emory University in Georgia he delivered an address about Evangelization and Church Growth in

Sangaya in Edinburgh, Scotland, 1961

Malawi (see appendix 4). He pointed out that the Blantyre Synod was committed to preaching the Gospel in areas of Malawi where the church had no presence such as Mangochi, Chikwawa and Mwanza. To achieve this, Sangaya said there was a need to emphasize leadership development, by cooperating with other Malawian churches and with partner churches overseas. Sangaya made such a deep impression on his audience at Emory University that they crowned him, "Dr Sangaya". Though Sangaya was not a doctor of any kind, he received a Doctor of Divinity, an honourary degree which any reputed University or Theological College may award to someone who has given distinctive service to one's country. Americans in Atlanta thus recognized the significant contribution made by Sangaya to the Church of Jesus Christ.

There is no doubt that he was a great church leader in Malawi and abroad. Tom Colvin's statement makes this clear:

> Sangaya became a missionary to white folks in his own land, in Scotland, England, the United States of America, and Canada, sharing with them his deep compassionate faith and knowledge of the Gospel

43

message of God's love. In himself he well represented that African understanding of the Gospel, which is so needed in these often inhuman and over-developed nations.

We have noted how Sangaya influenced the Blantyre Synod to express itself as an indigenous church by developing a strong leadership and a good and credible stewardship. As a result of this development, Blantyre Synod became self-reliant. Further, we have also noted that Sangaya made new contacts with churches and organizations in Africa and in the West. Through these contacts, Blantyre Synod was enhanced in its understanding of itself and its view of the church universal.

His Relationship with Missionaries

Sangaya had a dynamic relationship with Scottish missionaries within the Synod. The relationship developed from "servant" pupil to being in charge. Rev. Andrew Doig, who was Sangaya's predecessor, says,

> He [Sangaya] passed from the stage of being a pupil (even a servant)
> to being in charge, without losing his balance or sense of priorities.

Sangaya had to deal with older types of missionaries and newer ones. Most of the older types regarded themselves as masters and considered Malawians as their servants. To them Sangaya was only a servant with some capacity to grow. It was only after one had proved his worth that he was held with some respect. The newer ones were more supportive in their dealing with local people than those of the "master attitude" adopted by the older missionaries. To these newer missionaries, Sangaya was a promising church leader who deserved their support and a higher role than that of a "servant". Influenced by these two attitudes, Sangaya learned to be himself and to work peacefully with everyone.

We have already noted how quickly Sangaya rose from a village parish minister in 1952 to become General Secretary for Blantyre Synod in 1962. Sangaya was supportive of many missionaries. Miss Nita Douglas, who was Synod Treasurer during Sangaya's leadership, says,

> I liked Mr Sangaya very much indeed and found him easy to work
> with. He was easy to talk to; he would listen to any suggestions or
> complaints, and was always fair in his judgment. The work in the
> Treasurer's Department went smoothly while he was with us.

Another comment about Sangaya's supportive role was given by Rev. Alastair Rennie, saying, "His wish to cooperate for the benefit of the church and its departments had no sign of resentfulness. He seemed to like working with us."

Another person, Rev. Tom Colvin, says Sangaya encouraged the best in missionaries: "I loved Jonathan very much indeed, and my life is the richer for having shared much with him. I received so much from him." This brings out clearly that Sangaya was a loveable and dependable person and church leader.

Dr Andrew Ross, when talking about Sangaya today, still refers to him affectionately as "Bambo Sangaya", meaning Father Sangaya. There was something in his character which made those around him feel his love and concern. Ross remembers fondly that Sangaya often visited him and his family at Balaka. Every time there was an illness in the family, he was there to pray with them. Many missionary families, as well as Malawian families, would agree that Sangaya was a pastor at heart. This showed in his leadership and in his relationship with all people. It is clear that Sangaya's relationship with missionaries was that of mutual respect. Older missionaries considered Sangaya as a good student and someone they could trust. The newer missionaries regarded Sangaya as their leader, pastor and friend.

Missionaries Influence his Life

We have already noted how Sangaya, from his early years, was exposed to missionary teaching and their way of life. He attended Sunday School, went to a mission school and was under constant supervision by missionaries. Therefore it is clear that Sangaya was a product of missionary training and influence.

The prayerful life he had begun as a boy continued into his adulthood. The commitment he had seen among the missionaries was also to become his own. "He responded to the Gospel brought by missionaries, but discovered for himself that God was greater than the missionaries", commented Andrew Doig. We do not know for sure the names of all the missionaries who influenced Sangaya in his childhood. However, the fact that he later gave his first-born son the Scottish name of "McNeil" indicates a certain amount of missionary influence in his life.

In his adulthood, Sangaya was influenced by a number of missionaries. For example, Andrew Doig worked closely with Sangaya from 1960 to 1962, at the time when Doig was General Secretary and Member of Parliament representing missionary interests. Doig was considered by the Africans as a friend because of his opposition to laws which denigrated Africans and favoured Europeans. In his opposition to such laws, Doig used the Bible as his basis for argument. He believed that God created all humankind in his likeness, and that people of all races had equal rights and were to be given equal opportunities. From Doig, Sangaya learned how to combine true churchmanship with true statesmanship. He developed confidence in himself and knew that he was capable of bringing out the best in himself. It is not surprising that in his leadership of the church, as General Secretary, Sangaya sought to bring out the best in everyone.

Another missionary who influenced Sangaya was Rev. Tom Colvin. He first came to Malawi in 1954, when Sangaya was Assistant Minister to

Last meeting of Joint Council before handing over all powers to Blantyre Synod, 1958. From left: Rev. Andrew Doig, Rev. Tom Colvin, Rev. Frederick Chintali, Rev. Augustine Ndalama, Mr D.M. Mnkwaila, Rev. Charles Watt, Lester Chopi, Rev. H. Hepburn, Rev. S. Green, Mr Reid, Miss Nita Douglas, Rev. Andrew Ross, Rev. Alistair Rennie, (front) Rev. J.D. Sangaya, Mr M. Kumbikano, Rev. M.C. Matanda, Rev. S. Mliule.

Rev. Harry Kambwiri Matecheta of Bemvu in Ntcheu District. Colvin and Sangaya met from time to time whenever Colvin visited primary schools in to Ntcheu District and Bemvu. The two men developed a friendship which lasted all of Sangaya's life.

Colvin was a staunch supporter of African nationalists such as Sangaya, S. Somanje, Frederick Sangala and others who were struggling for political freedom for Nyasaland. Colvin encouraged them to engage in both political and spiritual liberation. His socialist tendencies made him popular among many Africans, but to his fellow Europeans, Colvin was an unwanted sell-out. When in 1955 Sangaya was transferred from Bemvu to Blantyre Mission, where he served as an Associate Minister at St Michael and All Angels church, he was provided with a golden opportunity to cultivate his friendship with Colvin. The two men saw each other often and shared ideas about church and political matters.

In 1958 the African Nyasaland Congress was at its peak in the mobilisation of mass protest against white rule, namely the Federation of Rhodesia and Nyasaland (FRN). The FRN had united what is now Malawi, Zambia and Zimbabwe with an aim of gaining Dominion status under white rule. Had this happened, it would have left Africans in these countries landless and politically powerless. This is why Africans opposed the Federation of Rhodesia and Nyasaland. Colvin and other sympathetic missionaries played an active role in siding with Malawian nationalists at that time. Sangaya, as Colvin's close friend, was following this political development. Colvin's position in politics resulted in his prohibition, thereby prematurely disrupting his friendship with Sangaya. Colvin went to Ghana, where he continued to correspond with Sangaya.

When Malawi became independent in 1964, the Federation also broke up. Colvin was recalled to Malawi by Sangaya, who was then General Secretary of Blantyre Synod. On 6th July, 1964, Colvin was honoured by being asked to offer a prayer of thanksgiving for the independence of Malawi during the celebration attended by over 40,000 people at Chichiri Stadium.

Sangaya went to Ghana to see the involvement of churches in development under an organisation called the Christian Service Committee, begun by Colvin when he was in that country. When Sangaya returned home, as already noted, he and Colvin formed the Christian Service Committee in

Malawi in 1968. The new organisation soon grew to include the Roman Catholic Church and 16 Protestant denominations. The aim of this organisation is to assist rural communities in uplifting their lives through self-help projects. For example, the CSC helped with the provision of clear, piped water, the building of bridges, health clinics and so forth. For many years Sangaya served as Chairman of the CSC while Colvin served as its Head of Programme.

The relationship between Colvin and Sangaya developed to such a level that it was one of mutual influence, sharing and caring. Colvin himself admits, "It was a unique relationship because so often Sangaya appeared to be asking me to help him, or share with him, in some enterprise or other. In fact, it was always I who was receiving the help, guidance and direction from him". The old Chichewa saying, "*Chitsulo chimanola chitsulo chinzake*", applies in the Colvin Sangaya relationship: "steel sharpens steel."

We have seen that Sangaya was influenced by Doig, Colvin and other missionaries with whom he worked and came into contact. His prayerful life and Christian dedication was shaped by those who taught him at school and those who worshipped with him throughout his life. All things considered, Sangaya was not what we term, a "yes bwana" type of man, i.e. a person who has no opinion of his own, but agrees about everything without reasoning for himself. Sangaya held his own opinions and projected his individuality, without bending the knee to anyone, in a way which obviated his own character and judgment. This won Sangaya much respect among missionaries and many other people, including those who were opposed to him.

His Religious Attitudes

Religious attitudes of an individual change due to experience, the influence of other people, reading, maturity, and so forth. We see changes in religious attitudes of many of the people we read about in the Bible, as well as those of people in our own times. Sangaya was not an exception to this understanding, as we have already noted some of the influences which came to bear upon him.

Sangaya's religious attitudes developed through experience, time, the influence of other people, age and reading. Those who knew him in his early Christian

48

life saw that there was nothing flamboyant about his approach. Faith, for Sangaya, was a real, childlike trust in a personal Saviour. This was later apparent in his evangelical preaching, when he said,

> Lowani pa chipata chopapatiza. Tikafuna chinthu cha mtengo wapatali, ndipo sitikhala a Khristu popanda kudzipereka. Potsegulira njira yopapatiza Yesu Mwana wa Mulungu anafika mwa chikondi ndipo adataya moyo wake, kuti ife tipulumuke titchedwe ana a Mulungu.

> [The translation reads:] Enter through the narrow gate. If we want something very precious, we cannot be Christians without giving ourselves up. Jesus the Son of God came in love to open the narrow way, and he gave up his life, so that we could be saved and called children of God.

In spite of seeing the light and moving in the right direction, Sangaya's faith was at first narrow and shaky. For example, in his early ministry Sangaya came through a very bad time. Before he was posted to Bemvu, he was drinking a lot. Then by the grace of God and his own effort, he overcame that problem. Like a wounded soldier, Sangaya became a greater helper and counsellor to many people who had drinking problems than he would otherwise have been.

Sangaya was a man in whom one could confide, utterly trusting his integrity. One could speak of one's fears and feelings and know he would advise, comfort and keep one's confidence to himself.

Later in his pilgrimage of faith Sangaya saw religion as always having practical consequences of personal, communal, and national nature. This is demonstrated in his sermon delivered on Martyr's Day in 1972, when he said, "We offer to God this day in silence our reverence, our humble remembrance of what other men and women were prepared to pay that we might live in peace."

Sangaya fostered his own spiritual life with Christian books and magazines. He often carried a new book to read in his briefcase for whenever he had a few minutes to himself. Some of his favourite authors were Stephen Neill, Max Weber, Reinhold Niebuhr, Kwesi Dickson, John Mbiti and many others. Often Sangaya would share his reading of a book with someone, thereby introducing the book to that person through conversation. Sangaya left behind a rich library which is at his farm at Namaka. We hope his family may want to honour him by donating, if not the whole library, then part of it, to Zomba Theological College.

Further, Sangaya enjoyed the radio ministry. While he often preached on Radio Malawi, he was also a keen listener of religious programmes on the Malawi Broadcasting Corporation (MBC). Rev. Josam Sankhani, Director of Religious Programmes at the MBC during Sangaya's time, said about him, "Even at the unearthly time of midnight, Sangaya would listen to the epilogues on MBC." Sangaya utilised this medium for his own spiritual growth and for sharing his faith with many people throughout the land.

Commenting on his devotional life, one person said:

> I found Sangaya very devout about, 'doing my Anglican prayer book' and reading from the Psalms. We often read them together with their strange Elizabethan English. The Psalms took on new meaning when so read by him.

Sangaya was not ashamed to share with other people his faith and joy in studying the word of God. For him, the Bible was the basis for his life and service.

Sangaya's own, and his family's, lifestyle was modest. He showed no desire for ostentatious appearance. This helped many ordinary people to approach him and feel comfortable in speaking to him. As a sign of this modesty, he held evening prayers every day with his family. He often asked his children and grandchildren to read the Bible in turn, while he always said the prayer. Sometimes he gave a short explanation on the passage read. Another sign of his modesty was his refusal to move to a bigger house on the mission. Sangaya never indulged in any outward show that might have put barriers between himself and others. This availability to people was a mark of the man's devotional life, and of his goodness and greatness.

His Death

Sangaya was in his house at Blantyre Mission on Sunday evening of the 22nd of June, 1979, when he phoned Toronto in Canada to speak to this writer who was in that far-off country on a six week official visit for the church. On that Sunday, Sangaya and Rev. Jonathan Kadawati had just returned from a two day preaching engagement at Nsanje, a mosquito breeding belt in Malawi. Sangaya had gone to Nsanje in spite of his ill health at that time. He was recovering from an appendectomy and was suffering from high blood pressure, but what was important to Sangaya was to minister to these people who needed his help, not to nurse his own problem. When he returned from Nsanje, Sangaya's health deteriorated, maybe due to the long distance; perhaps he had overworked. On the phone to Toronto, Sangaya's voice was faint and tired. It was punctuated by heavy breathing.

No one who knew Sangaya's usual musical voice on the phone would have missed that he was unwell. Therefore, this writer knew from the voice that the old man was sick. He, however, wanted to know when this writer would return to Malawi. I replied, "in another three weeks time." At that time we (my wife and I) wondered why he wanted to know the date for our return, as this was already known to him. We will look at this point later. Here it is enough to say that we communicated with Sangaya and we knew he was sick even though he did not say so himself.

Sangaya was treated and had his high blood pressure checked by Dr F. Kidy, after which he recovered to fulfill his July engagements. On 6th July 1979, he was at Kwacha International Conference Center for a National Service of Worship to mark Independence Day. The following Sundays in the same month, Sangaya preached in different village churches, encouraging the local people in their faith. Further, Sangaya met with many individuals during that month who, in reflection after his death, wondered if Sangaya had known about his imminent death.

If anything can be said about this servant of God, it is that he knew that his physical body was weak and losing its energy. He seemed prepared to depart from this world. To K.C. Matupa, one of his students at Henry Henderson Institute, and later on one of his elders and reliable friends, he said, "We have now completed repairing St Michael and All Angels Church. I had feared that it would fall in my time. God has helped us to do the repair work well. If I die now, I will die in peace". When Sangaya said these words to Matupa, they did not mean much to him then, but three weeks later when Sangaya died, his words echoed in Matupa's mind and brought new meaning. The words now meant that Sangaya had satisfactorily completed his task of handing over the church to the next generation, and that gave him a peace of mind for his departure from this world. At another occasion during this same period, Sangaya also spoke to one of the younger ministers, Rev. Misanjo Kansilanga, saying, "For a long time our Synod had resented having young ministers on its role, but today I am so glad that there are so many of you. It is you young ministers who will carry on with the work of the church when we old ones go. In fact, I have little time before my time expires". Kansilanga was surprised when Sangaya's time expired only a few days after he had talked with him.

It is interesting to observe that Sangaya's last words to people were words of encouragement. To all those he met and spoke, he admonished them and urged them to carry on the Lord's work and to be strong in the faith. Rev. Harry Ngwale was right when he said that Sangaya was being transformed into a saint by God while we were watching. In his later years, Sangaya was adorned with beautiful grey hair which gave him a saintly look.

Knowingly or unknowingly, in the last few weeks of his life, Sangaya was handing over the torch to those who would remain working in God's vineyard. At the same time, Sangaya was saying a simple and loving goodbye to his friends, workmates and to all who had encouraged him and worshipped with him on his spiritual journey.

In the first week of July, 1979, Sangaya was admitted to Queen Elizabeth Hospital in Blantyre. His blood pressure was high, he had a high fever, and his earlier gall-bladder operation had not healed well. His breathing was heavy, and he was exhausted. His wife, Christian, was at his bedside when Rev. Bauleni Akule visited Sangaya at the Hospital in Block 28, side ward 2. Sangaya was cheerful as he chatted with Akule about many things regarding the work of the church. What remains clear in Akule's memory about his visit were Sangaya's last words to him. "This time I will not walk out of this place alive because the roots of the tree have been cut and the tree must soon fall." Sangaya referred to himself as a tree which was soon to fall. What was he seeing ahead and behind him?

On the 15th of July, Sangaya had a dream. He dreamt first of seeing a flock of sheep without a shepherd. Then he dreamt of seeing a pair of shoes without an owner. Sangaya gave the interpretation of his dream to his wife and also to Rev. H. Sindima. He said he saw in this vision the people of God in the Synod of Blantyre without a leader. All along, including on his death bed, Sangaya's concern was for other people. He wanted the church to continue after him under able leadership. Was that leadership available? This is a subject of its own. Here it is enough to say that Sangaya had trained a number of ministers who would be able to lead the church into the future, but there was no apparent heir to his position.

On Sunday morning at 7:00 a.m., the 22nd of July, Sangaya died peacefully in the hands of his wife, Christian. He died on the Lord's Day when the church he loved and served for most of his life was awake to praise God in singing, prayer and hearing the word of God. This great servant of God, who had toiled in his Master's vineyard, went to eternal rest, finally satisfied that he had fought the good fight.

On the same day that Sangaya died, this writer received a phone call while still in Canada announcing the death of the "big man". Upon receiving that phone call from Rev. Charles Scott, this writer reflected on the earlier phone call Sangaya had made to Canada when he returned from his pastoral visit to Nsanje. The purpose of Sangaya's phone call to Canada on 22nd June, 1979, had been to find out when this writer would return to Malawi, as already noted. We had left Malawi on 3rd June, and had been in Canada barely three weeks. It would seem that Sangaya had either forgotten that we were to be away for six weeks, or had sensed his impending death and wanted this writer back home to ensure that church work continued well after his death!? The latter seems to have been the case. Sangaya was fully committed to his work. He loved the Synod of Blantyre and carried its burden in his life. He worked to see that the whole church grew in its various aspects of preaching the Gospel of Jesus Christ and giving service to all people.

He also wanted the church to continue doing well after his departure. He said during one of the Synod meetings, "When I retire, I want the church to be led by people who understand the meaning of the word *church*." Sangaya's retirement was to be spent in heaven – he did not linger around. To ensure that the church would continue to be led by such people of understanding, Sangaya invested confidence, trust and education in a number of promising young leaders and young ordained ministers, as was already noted.

It is not surprising that after Sangaya's death, a group of younger ministers were elected to positions in the church. First, the immediate problem with which the Synod was faced after Sangaya's death was, "How does the Synod appoint a General Secretary?" The Synod had received Sangaya as its General Secretary upon the recommendation of missionaries who had long ago returned to Scotland. There was much debate as to the issue of appointing a new General Secretary. Finally this writer was recalled from Canada to lead the Synod in making its decision about appointing a new General Secretary. As Acting General Secretary for three months, i.e. August to October, this writer made all the necessary arrangements for the election of the new General Secretary. The Synod meeting for this purpose was held at Chilema in October 1979. At that meeting a group of younger ministers were elected to top positions in the church. Rev. B.A. Kuntembwe was elected Synod Moderator. Rev. Dr S.D. Chiphangwi was elected General Secretary, and this writer continued as Deputy General Secretary. Sangaya rests satisfied that his wish that the church accept young leadership was fulfilled, and continues to be respected to this day.

Rumours about Sangaya's Death

It is rumoured that Sangaya did not die a natural death, but that Kamuzu Banda ordered him beaten. Consequently, Sangaya died at Queen Elizabeth Central Hospital. According to the rumour, Sangaya was beaten because, in the early 1970s, he suggested a marriage between Kamuzu Banda and Mama Cecilia Tamanda Kadzamira who had been cohabiting with him for many years. Supposedly, Sangaya's Calvinistic piety could not tolerate seeing an old bachelor and a single woman living together in the same house without falling into temptation. To solve the problem, the two people had to marry, even if the ceremony had to be strictly private. So, his suggestion for a marriage was a provocation to Kamuzu Banda whose ego was so strong that he never took kindly to criticism. No wonder, goes the rumour, Sangaya was flogged resulting in his death. The other side of the same rumour says that Kamuzu Banda and Cecilia Kadzamira accepted Sangaya's suggestion for a marriage between them. Sangaya joined the couple and issued them with an official certificate. The rumour goes on to say that it was the production of that marriage certificate in 1997 that made Kadzamira jump the line of mourners from behind to be the chief mourner at Kamuzu Banda's funeral. Though Kadzamira did not produce the said certificate in court to claim the inheritance of Dr Banda's property, the rumour says that on its strength her claim was legitimised. The second rumour about Sangaya's death says that he asked one of the clergy from Nkhoma Synod of the CCAP to perform the wedding at Sanjika palace. Again, this was in the 1970s. The wedding was acted. But, after the cleric returned home, he lost his life in a mysterious way. Soon after that cleric died, Sangaya also died having been beaten.

In Malawi some rumours are mere speculation and are meant to entertain the hearers and arouse their imagination. Yet some rumours carry with them specks of factual events. So, one should not completely ignore rumours, but sift them to find what is true. When this writer interviewed Mrs Sangaya and her daughter Eleanor, one thing was certain about Sangaya's death. Both mother and daughter said:

> If the MCP functionaries had beaten him [Sangaya], he would have told us without fail. He told us about how well the Commissioner of Police Kamwana treated him after his arrest when he returned from Zambia. The police released him after three days, though some MCP had wished him punished. He told us about this experience. Why would he now hide a secret beating meant to end his life?

Sangaya's family doctor was Dr Bauxtine at Queen Elizabeth Hospital. If he as family doctor had diagnosed something on Sangaya, Dr Bauxtine would have asked Mrs Sangaya to explain, but nothing of that sort arose. Therefore, this writer believes the story told by Sangaya's wife and daughter. Sangaya may have been beaten at one time by MCP functionaries. This would not be surprising as it used to happen to many people in Malawi. But, Sangaya did not die of inflicted injuries.

What is interesting about the above rumour is, indeed, was Banda officially married to Kadzamira? This writer lived through the whole of Banda's reign and observed, from a dangerous distance, the relational changes between Kamuzu and Kadzamira. In 1961 when Banda came back from Gweru in Zimbabwe where he and other Malawians were imprisoned, Kadzamira was his private nurse who had formerly worked with him in his Limbe surgery. So, it was not strange for Dr Banda to have chosen Kadzamira as his private nurse, especially since he was in his fifties and single. Soon after independence, it was necessary for Kadzamira to become *Official Hostess*. In that position, she fulfilled the First Lady's duties because Kamuzu Banda received and entertained many important visitors. Though she filled that role,

Kadzamira remained in the background and initially she did not live under the same roof as the President. In the 1970s Cecilia Kadzamira became *Mama* with a capital M, signifying that she was the *First Mother of Malawi*. Now, President Banda could not address the public without saying, *Mama and I are very happy to see you my people*. Further, all presidential invitations now read as follows, His Excellency Ngwazi Dr H. Kamuzu Banda Life President of the Republic of Malawi and *Mama C. Tamanda Kadzamira* invite you...

In public, Cecilia Kadzamira occupied a prominent position. Her seat was always next to that of the President. When one greeted the President by shaking hands, Kamuzu Banda made sure, jerking your hand towards Cecilia, that you also shake *Mama's* hand. Even cabinet ministers paid their courtesy to her, a sign that she carried more authority than they did. Kadzamira was in full control at Sanjika Palace. Visitors to the Palace always met both the President and Mama though she did not participate in the discussions. Her presence could not be ignored. In their secrets of secrets, President Banda could not go to his bedroom located on the western part of the house without passing through Kadzamira's bedroom. The arrangements of the bedrooms were such that a corridor led into *Mama's* bedroom and an open door from there led into the Big Man's large bedroom. This closeness knitted Banda and Kadzamira with a matrimonial flavour. Workers around and inside the Palace were more afraid of Mama Kadzamira than they were of the President. As Mama, she had the final word. One worker at Sanjika Palace said, "If you cross Mama's wrong side, you know that you are in for big trouble." Apparently the relationship between President Banda and Cecilia Kadzamira developed from a master/aid to a lasting companionship and possibly to a marriage. No one has yet seen the marriage certificate between Banda and Kadzamira signed by either Sangaya or the unknown cleric from Nkhoma Synod. We might have had two angels living together at Sanjika palace for thirty years, who knows?

His Burial

On 24th July, 1979, the day when Sangaya was buried, Queen Elizabeth II of the United Kingdom was visiting Malawi. On that particular day the Queen was travelling by road from Zomba, the then Capital City, to Blantyre. We mention this because Sangaya's body, which had been carried the previous day from Queen Elizabeth Hospital in Blantyre to his farm in Namaka, was being driven on the same day and on the same Zomba-Blantyre road the Queen was to pass through. There were literally thousands of people lined up along that route to see and cheer the Queen. When the hearse, with police escort plus a fleet of cars, carried Sangaya's body on its way from Namaka to Blantyre, some people along the road mistakenly clapped their hands and raised their hand flags thinking that it was the Queen and her convoy. Though it was a sad procession for Sangaya's funeral, Sangaya received from the crowds along the road rousing royal cheers on his way to St Michael and All Angels Church for the funeral service. This was as if both heaven and earth were rejoicing that Sangaya had successfully completed his mission and was now raised on high to join the saints.

At St Michael and All Angels Church in Blantyre, Sangaya's funeral service was conducted by the Rev. Dr Saindi Chiphangwi. In his homily he said that one of the strong pillars which held the Synod of Blantyre together had fallen and could hardly be replaced. It is true that Sangaya's whole life was interwoven with the Synod of Blantyre. During his lifetime it was not possible to think of Blantyre Synod without Sangaya. We have already noted that he worked for the church and defended it with his life when it was necessary to do so. Other ministers who participated in the funeral service included Rev. Cedric Nkunga, the Synod Moderator, Rev. Gibson Kazembe, and Rev. Simon Faiti.

The burial service followed immediately at Blantyre Mission graveyard. Sangaya was buried in the third row on the left side as one enters the cemetery through the main gate. The burial service was conducted by the Rev. Cedric Nkunga. Many Mvano women decorated the closed grave with beautiful flowers to mark the end of Sangaya's earthly life. As an ex-serviceman, Sangaya also received a military salute at the graveyard. The army paid its last tribute to Sangaya with a gun salute. It was right to honour this old soldier this way. Sangaya was a brave fighter both in the battle field and in the church.

It was estimated that about three thousand people attended Sangaya's funeral. Many dignitaries were among the crowd. The Life President, Ngwazi Dr H. Kamuzu Banda, was represented by Mr Bakili Muluzi, the Minister without

Portfolio and Administrative Secretary of the Malawi Congress Party (MCP). Mr Muluzi spoke on behalf of His Excellency the President saying that the sudden death of the Very Rev. Jonathan Sangaya had shocked him deeply. Muluzi went on to say that had the Queen completed her visit and left the country, the President would have wanted to be at Sangaya's funeral. Dr Banda had never attended anyone's funeral, and for him to have wished to attend in person Sangaya's funeral says much about Sangaya. If the burial of Sangaya had not coincided with the visit of the Queen, Sangaya's funeral would have been the biggest ever to have taken place in Malawi. There is no doubt that Sangaya was a respectable and responsible citizen of Malawi. He was an ecumenist, a strong church leader and a servant of God.

On his tombstone, and on a plaque placed in the front right of St Michael and All Angels Church, is an inscription, "The Very Rev. Jonathan Sangaya, The First African General Secretary of the Synod of Blantyre." Underneath these words is a quotation from 2 Timothy 4:7,

> I have fought the good fight, I have finished the race, I have kept the faith.

We indeed remember Sangaya, as a soldier for Christ, who, after he had faithfully served his Master and his fellow human beings, was called by God to the highest glory, where he now rests in the company of Abraham, Harry Matecheta and all the saints. Let us strive on in our pilgrimage of faith and service to follow the example of people like Sangaya.

Nkhoma Synod regrets death of Rev. Sangaya. May God comfort bereaved family.

General Secretary, Nkhoma Synod

We mourn with you on loss of Very Rev. Sangaya STOP Revelation 14:13
Peter Kodjko, Africa Secretary, World Student Christian Federation

It was with deep regret that we received the cable from Charles Scott informing us of the passing of our brother and colleague, the Very Rev. Jonathan Sangaya. We immediately sent you the following cable.

All my colleagues here in New York who had the joy of getting acquainted with Jonathan Sangaya during his visit here were very sorry to hear the news of his passing. We were all, however, conscious of the fact that he had been through a very difficult time physically and that his being called home to be with the Lord had probably been a very great release for him, even though a great loss for his family and for the Synod.

L. Paul Hopkins, Liaison with Africa, Presbyterian Church (USA)

I was too sad to hear from Edinburgh yesterday of the passing of my old friend Rev. J.D. Sangaya. May I express my sympathy with you and your Synod, and ask you to give our assurance of prayer and consolation to his widow and family.

W.H. Watson, Minister, Salisbury Presbyterian Church

Deepest sympathy with your sad loss of Reverend Sangaya. STOP We thank God for his leadership of the Theological Board. STOP May the Lord comfort you.

Human, Secretary for Theological Board

Overseas Board of Presbyterian Church in Ireland sends deepest sympathy on death of Very Rev. J.D. Sangaya.

Young, Presbyterian Church in Ireland

On behalf of my church I am writing to let you know how very, very sad we are to hear of the death of Rev. J. Sangaya, the man of God. I thank the Lord for the Life and Ministry of Rev. Sangaya which he did both for the Blantyre Synod of the CCAP and other denominations within and outside

Malawi. I am sure when he stood in the presence of our Lord Jesus Christ he heard the welcome word of our Lord Jesus Christ, "Well done servant ..."

P. Goba, General Secretary, Africa Evangelical Church

We have just learned of the death of the Very Rev. J.D. Sangaya. On behalf of the Presbyterian Church in Canada I would like to express to you our deepest sympathy and an assurance of how deeply we mourn with you.

A few of our people have had the rich privilege of visiting Malawi and getting to know Mr Sangaya in the midst of the country and church which he so deeply loved. Many more Canadian Presbyterians came to know him through his visit to Canada and his sharing of Christian faith and dedication in many of our congregations. All of us felt a deep warmth for him and a thankfulness to God that we were allowed to share with his servant J.D. Sangaya.

Earle Roberts, Overseas Operations, Presbyterian Church in Canada

I and my colleagues of the Embassy of the Republic of China are deeply grieved in hearing the Very Rev. Sangaya has passed away on Sunday, July 22. It is hoped that our sincere condolences be conveyed to the bereaved of the Very Rev. Sangaya.

His Excellency C.Y Chao, Ambassador of the People's Republic of China

Moderator of Livingstonia Synod and whole Synod regret death of Right Rev. Sangaya.

W. Jere, Moderator, Livingstonia Synod

Salisbury Synod is deeply shocked to hear about the passing of Rev.erend Sangaya. Please extend our heartfelt sympathy to family members and Synod.

Clerk of Synod, Salisbury Synod, Church of Central Africa Presbyterian

Please accept our profoundest deepest sympathies, the same to his family on behalf of the writer and his family, at a very untimely sad demise of late Rev. Sangaya.

May his soul rest in peace, and may God grant the family interminable courage to face this unforeseen circumstance.

He would always be remembered as a very warm and gregarious person, with a smile in every vicissitude of life, and endless kindness which he has portrayed during his lifetime. His tireless task of serving the needy will be like a shining beacon for years to come, with silent prayers being offered from dawn to dusk, he shall be remembered by people of all walks of life.

B.C. Desai, Manager, Joint Agencies

We have learnt with deep sorrow the passing away of our friend and brother Rev. Sangaya. Please accept on behalf of the AACC and on my own behalf our heartfelt condolences. We pray for you at this time and may God rise yet another servant in Malawi. God's richest blessings,

Kodwo Ankrah, General Secretary, All Africa Conference of Churches

The news of Mr Sangaya's death arrived while I was on holiday. Colleagues did, however, let me know this sad news at once and a letter was sent to all missionaries who had served with Blantyre Synod. I would like to convey to you, and the Synod, the sincere sympathy of the Overseas Council during this time of sadness and loss. Mr Sangaya's life was the church, and therefore, it was not surprising that his call to higher services should come while he was still on active service.

I was glad I had the opportunity of meeting Mr Sangaya in Malawi as well as in Scotland. Although he was an administrator for many years, he never lost contact with the people at the local congregational level. I shall always remember the day when he took me to visit the Mpasa Congregation. His contact and communication with the congregation was quite amazing.

Later in the day we visited Likhubula and then went to the Mulanje Hospital. After we left the Likhubula road and turned on to the main road, the Landrover could not get up the hill with all of us on board. It had been raining heavily. Mr Sangaya and I had many laughs as we struggled through the mud, arm in arm. He survived the long tiring day in a most remarkable way.

I am glad, too, that we had the privilege of entertaining Mr Sangaya in our own home in Edinburgh when he returned from America last year. Former missionaries came to meet him and it was very obvious how deeply all respected him.

We assure you of our prayers at this time and join with you in giving thanks for the life of Jonathan Sangaya and for the outstanding contribution he has made to the life of the Church in Malawi.

Ian Moir, Executive Secretary,
Overseas Council of the Church of Scotland

A Letter Regarding the Need to Care for Retired Ministers

General Secretary's Office
Box 413
Blantyre.

April 3, 1976

To: All Ministers,
     Blantyre Synod.

Dear Sirs:

Remembering Our Retired Ministers

Two letters from two of our retired ministers recently left me a bad conscience. How easily have we shelved and forgotten the lives and great contributions of our retired ministers who have worked in the church, community and among us, I thought to myself. This is what has prompted me to write this circular.

In its true sense, retirement is a glorious stage of development in one's life when one looks back, with joy, to see the fruits of one's many years of service. It is a time when one looks forward with hope to the fulfilment of life in Jesus Christ, the same yesterday, today and tomorrow. It is also a time of change when one realises one's physical weariness. In all, retirement is a victorious age.

The needs of a retired minister are legion. At the time of retirement, the acute problem which comes is that of a home. A minister who has lived in a church manse almost all of his life is suddenly confronted with the big question - *Where do I go*? The ever-rising cost of living and the inadequate stipends which ministers get make saving money almost impossible and retirement unthinkable and unwelcome. This is why our Synod has a small revolving fund to loan those ministers who wish to build a home of their own in preparation for retirement.

Last year I was deeply moved by the warm welcome with which I was received at one of our retired minister's home. Behind the cheerful face of this minister, I observed a need for belonging and a sense of fellowship which my presence brought. Otherwise this minister felt cast out and forgotten. My presence assured the old minister that he was remembered and still belonged to a group. My dear friends, a visit to a retired minister's home is one of the noble gestures of brotherhood which each one of us should do at least once a year. By doing so we show our thankfulness to those who trod on the same path on which we now walk.

A retired minister is like a living and moving encyclopaedia. In him is embedded the wisdom of the past. His long experience is parallel with the richness in ideas which he has gathered over the years. We may lose this valuable treasure if all of us who are young keep away from the old people.

The church too should utilise the experience of the old servicemen who have given all their lives to its service. Although some of them may not be able to come, it should be a sign of remembering our retired ministers to invite them to our Presbytery and Synod meetings. Some may feel strong enough to preach a Christmas sermon each year and some may be able to write their ideas about current issues in the church. Why should we cut the throats and hands of our old people? Retired ministers are intellectually, spiritually and socially alive, especially, if we encourage them to stay alive and active. Let us remember our retired ministers by giving them a sense of belonging to the community, by giving them information about what is going on in the church and by giving them our love and care. In Hebrews 13:7 we are reminded thus: *"Remember your former leaders who spoke God's message to you. Think back on how they lived, and imitate their faith."*

Yours sincerely
Very Rev. J.D. Sangaya
GENERAL SECRETARY

Appendix 3
Letters of recommendation

Church of Scotland Mission
Blantyre.

31st January, 1933.

This is to certify that Jonathan Douglas has been in the service of the Blantyre Mission as a Teacher since the completion of his training in 1929.

As a member of the Teaching Staff of the Henry Henderson Institute he has given every satisfaction in the faithful discharge of his duties. He is eminently capable and trustworthy. He has no cause to give up his teaching career as a member of the Institute Staff and his resignation is disappointing.

Training & Qualifications: Jonathan Douglas was educated at the Henry Henderson Institute and completed his training as a teacher in 1929, gaining a Second Class Certificate. In 1930 he qualified to be registered as First Grade Certificated Teacher (Department of Education, Nyasaland).

Richard Paterson.

Henry Henderson Institute
Church of Scotland Mission
Blantyre
Nyasaland.

10th April, 1943.

To whom it may concern,

Jonathan Douglas Sangaya leaves school to join the Army Education Corps. He has given diligent service to this mission as a teacher over a period of some seventeen years during which time his work has been very satisfactory indeed. Not only in routine school work but in his many activities outwith the working day he has shown willingness and enthusiasm.

He is an elder of the Church of Central Africa Presbyterian and very upright fellow.

He holds the Nyasaland Government English Teachers' Certificate.

G. Hall
HEADMASTER.

To whoever it may concern.

Sgt Jonathan Sangaya served under my command for six months in 1945 as Sgt in charge of Education. During this time he was responsible for the education of the Asikari and also taught newly arrived Europeans. He has proved himself to be a first class instructor. He has also been in charge of the African Canteen and has shown great powers of organisation.

His knowledge of English is excellent and I can recommend him as a first class fellow who is capable of holding responsible positions.

Capt. O.C. Adm. Coy. 14 (Ny) KAR. 16 Aug. 45.

Testimonial

No.- DN. 17476. Rank. W.O.II. Name:- Jonathan Sangaya. S.G. 22

General Behaviour:- Excellent.
Diligence of Work: - Excellent.
Personal Appearance: - Clean Smart and Soldierly.
Teaching Personality: - Well above Average.
Initiative: - Excellent. Has run Educational side of Dispersal Centre for 6 months.
Any special qualifications for post war employment:-
Passed Ist. Grade government English certificate. Trained as a Teacher at Blantyre Scottish Mission. Passed Standard VI. An excellent type of African whom I was very sorry to lose from my staff.

Major. Commanding, Dispersal Centre, Ntondwe, Nyasaland.

To whom it may concern

During most of his service in the East Africa Army Education Corps, Mr Jonathan D. Sangaya was in my area, attached to the 14th (Nyasaland) Battalion, The King's African Rifles. He was later employed as Senior Education and Welfare Warrant Officer at Ntondwe Dispersal Centre.

During his service I came to regard him as one of the best African NCOs or WOs who had served with me. He is a good instructor, a reliable and responsible supervisor of his juniors, and a man who commands respects among his own people and soon earned it from his officers. I have no hesitation in recommending him for any appointment in which such a combination of qualities is required.

(Late major, Deputy Asst. Director of Education and Welfare, Southern Area, East African Command).

Appendix 4
Meditations by Sangaya

Revelation 8:1

> And when he had opened the seventh seal, there was silence in
> heaven about the space of half an hour.

No one, young or old, can fail to be impressed by the two minutes of silence
on successive *Remembrance Days*. These are moments when many look back
to the first Armistice Day, when the last guns fell silent. For all, it is a time
for looking around the world to other similar groups of people observing the
same silence, and forming a chain of fellowship in remembering.

In this text we are directed and helped to look into heaven; "there was
silence in heaven". The silence was due to shouts of victors and praises of
the redeemed. God could not hear something. He had prayers of people
still on earth. How long? Suffering, afraid of what was going to happen. If
we set aside these two minutes for God to speak to us, how much longer
will it take for him to listen, to hear and to accept what we have to say to
him in reverent silence from our hearts on such a day?

1. We offer to God this day in silence our reverent, humble remembrance
of what other men and women were prepared to pay that we might live. In
Malawi, we remember 1914-1918, how our people at Songaya lost their
lives, and 1939-1945 when many people lost their lives in Somaliland and
in British Malaysia. In Malawi in 1959 many people lost their lives for the
fight of freedom.

This peace we still enjoy; this freedom which is ours: the lives of children
both unshadowed by fear - none of these are our own, they were bought
with a price.

2. We offer to God in reverent silence our prayers for those who still suf-
fer, and for the lost and frightened as well in a frightening world. Sometimes we fight, till poppies bring their reminder, not only of those who
died, but also the living, who still pay a price. Some lost their health, such
as those at Zomba "wounded location", a housing scheme for wounded
soldiers; some of them are with us here today.

The ordinary man does not want war - of course he is always the loser from it, but he can be led to believe that he needs it, or war may be forced upon him. It is clear that we cannot save ourselves without God. The very agony we share with the ordinary man everywhere must form a prayer crying out in the silence of this day. How do we know God will hear and answer? The cross of Jesus Christ is the symbol and measure of God's caring which is set over the graves of the fallen.

We offer to God, in the silence, our dedication to the tasks and duties that lie before us. There may not be much the ordinary man can do to influence the course of world events, but it is a challenge to show in his daily life the kind of spirit ordinary folk, young and old alike, showed during the testing years of war, the spirit of peacemaking.

Always we have a struggle between good and evil, and second best, between selfishness and service. We must all in this reverent silence, with the hosts of heaven about us, dedicate ourselves. We dare not do less. There is but one gift that all our dead desire, that God make us better men.

Luke 23:34

Father forgive them for they know not what they do

These words were spoken by our dear Lord Jesus Christ while he was being nailed on the Cross. This is a prayer which Christ prayed for the people and for the soldiers who were concerned in his crucifixion. In this prayer Christ is asking his Farther to forgive them. So we learn by the Cross of Christ the unspeakable love of God for us all.

The first thing we learn about the Cross is that Jesus Christ is revealing the Love of God for all people upon the earth. Here too the Cross demonstrated how horrible sin is in its effects. It hates; it kills; it ignores the love of God by condemning the only sinless son of men and Son of God When we lift our eyes and look at the Cross, We Christians should be touched by the Love of God, because it will remind us of our sinful state.

"When I survey the wondrous cross on which the Prince of Glory died ... Love so amazing, so divine, demands my soul, my life, my all." Do we feel like that? It is for each one of us to think about.

The second thing we learn from these words is that Jesus declared that his work was to redeem the souls of all the people on earth, with no distinction of colour or of language.

"And I, if I be lifted up, will draw all men unto me" (John 12:32). It is while he is drawing all the people to himself that we hear these graceful words, "Father forgive them". I don't think you will find in the early history of mankind a sentence such as this. It was on the Cross that the work of atonement was done. If we despise the Cross we shall indeed lose the way of salvation. There can be no excuse for us. No saying that we did not know.

We know how the Jews missed salvation, missed forgiveness. It was because they thought that being the chosen people, they were therefore holy. Do we perhaps say that we really don't need to experience forgiveness anew, because we were once baptized into the Christian faith? If we say that we have no sin we deceive ourselves and the truth is not in us. If we confess our sins, He is faithful and just to forgive us our sins and to cleanse us from all unrighteousness.

"If we say we have not sinned we make Him a liar and His Word is not in us" (I John 1:10). Are we ready to confess now? This is the day, this is the time. Now...

In connection with forgiveness we should consider what Jesus actually taught about it. He says,

> For if ye forgive men their trespasses, your heavenly Father will also forgive you, but if you forgive not men their trespasses neither will your Father forgive your trespasses" (Matthew 6:14-15).

This does not mean God keeps an exact count of how much we forgive men their trespasses. He is not an exacting taskmaster, but he does require from us the spirit of forgiveness, the willingness to forgive others. Because only so can our personal relations between ourselves and God, and ourselves and other people, be established. Resentment creates a barrier between ourselves and the love of God through which His healing grace penetrates.

This means too that we must be ready to face and confess our known sins, and having done that it is our duty to accept forgiveness for ourselves which enables us to walk in newness of life. Walking in newness of life means that a man has really repented: that he has changed his direction, and that people can see the evidence of this.

Is this what forgiveness means for you? Is forgiveness a reality for you in the terms which Jesus laid down?

The third thing we learn from Jesus' prayer on the cross is how sin has established its government in the hearts of men and women. Mankind rebelled against God's Kingdom and so lost its divine state.

It was the rebel government that Jesus came to destroy, and to restore God's Kingdom. It was not an easy job to reconcile the rebels back to God. It needed a spotless lamb for an acceptable sacrifice.

Jesus gave himself, his body and soul, and suffered willingly for our salvation. He was numbered with the transgressors, and he bore the sins of many and made intercession for the transgressors.

We ourselves, as well as the whole of mankind, were numbered with Christ in his death, and at the cross we receive remission of our sins. Knowing this, that the rebellious state in us is crucified with Him, and that the body of sin might be destroyed, then henceforth we should not serve sin. The Cross still stands unchanged today. Every day we Christians stand face to face with God's love.

Can't we make the surrender today? Are we not yet sure that those who truly confess their sins are being forgiven? Let me tell you a story of what happened to my brother. Some thirty years ago he was working in a printing office, and he had a master who was very good to him. My brother had an idea that he could grow some tobacco to increase his income. Since his father was retired, he thought that his father could look after the crops, while he continued to work at the printing office.

But how was he to get the money? Well, he went to his boss, explained the scheme, and he got a loan of money to start him off on his tobacco farm. The first season was not very good, the second was no better, but my brother kept hoping that one day things would be all right and he would be able to repay the debt. But things did not get better. All the money was gone and he was a very worried man, wondering how he was going to face his employer. He became thin, and people used to wonder what was happening to him.

Soon came the time for the master to retire from the printing works, and one day he sent for my brother. "Go", he said to him, "and bring all the invoices and statements in connection with your business on the tobacco farm". When he brought them to him, his employer took them and tore them up in front of him. "Now", said the master, "you are free. You are at liberty once more. Your debts are all cancelled." My brother could scarcely believe his good fortune.

He called his friends for a feast, and they all marvelled at his changed appearance. Soon he was a carefree man once more. The burden of his debt was lifted. He was at liberty once more. God is doing the same through Jesus Christ for us.

He says to each one of us, "Produce your statement of account and all your invoices. The whole debit balance of your sins." He will destroy them all, and you will be free!

Father, forgive them ...

Psalms 1:1

> Blessed is the man that walketh not in the council of [the] ungodly,
> nor standeth in the way of sinners nor sitteth in the seat of the
> scornful.

This book of Psalms opens with a benediction, "Blessed", as did the famous sermon of our Lord upon the mountain.

Here we hear instructions which are given to a traveller so that he does not go astray. The instructions are given to an individual therefore each of us are in the arena. Every trip or journey has is cause and it has its difficulties and hindrances. So the Psalmist is warning us beforehand.

1. He walketh not in the council of the ungodly.

He takes wiser council and walks in the commandments of the Lord his God.

We are spoiled by the company [we] associate with and we hear such idioms [as] a bird of one feather together. We should always ask ourselves, "Is this a good company I walk with?" Many a man have been ruined in life by associating themselves to walking with [the] ungodly. Thou shalt not follow a multitude to do evil. It is not quantity that matters but quality.

Our footsteps should be ordered by the word of God and not by the cunning and wicked devices of carnal men.

It is a rich sign of inward grace when the outward walk is changed, and when ungodly is put far from our actions.

2. Nor standeth in the ways of the sinners.

Sins have great influence. Many people can be deceived by thinking that merely standing watching evil doers cannot affect them. That is not true.

Our eyes are like cameras, they take pictures, develop them, and if the objects we see are evil, we shall soon be influenced.

Many young men and young women have lost their future, Why? Because they have been standing in wrong places. The advice is that such places should be avoided. Always stand at a place where blessings can be bestowed.

3. Nor sitteth in the seat of [the] scornful.

Many places now are spoiled by scornful people. Some despise God in their talks, laugh at people who go to worship God. Some rich and scornful people usually say why go to church and worship God we have nothing to beg we have everything we don't need God. Jesus always [says], If any man wish to come after me must deny himself, and take his cross daily and follow Him.

We find a blessed life to Jesus Christ. If we have been walking, standing and sitting in places of that nature, let us receive this advice from the Bible.

My presence here is a living parable of love. Through God's love revealed to us in Jesus Christ our Lord, you and I are able to meet and share the joy and fruits of the Cross and the Risen Christ.

I wonder what you think and feel when you hear this word *Evangelism*. To me it denotes the Church of Jesus throughout the world in action - action proclaiming the Good News of Salvation. Our confession of Christ as Lord does not take His Church to the clouds. Instead it brings the Church down to earth and face to face with our day to day lives. This means that *Evangelism* and *Renewal* is concerned with how we treat and live with one another, how we govern our countries; how we share food and natural resources in the world that God has given us. In this sense *Evangelism* is treading in the dangerous path which our Lord Jesus passed through even to death.

Through *Evangelism* the Church in the world is called to confess Jesus Christ as the one Lord for us all. Through *Evangelism* the Church is called to unify the whole world, torn by racial, religious, political and ideological differences, to be one family - "the family of God". Hereby we today stand by the faithful witness of the Gospel throughout the ages and agree with our brother Paul that to confess Christ as Lord is no easy task (2 Cor. 4:7-11): "*Yet we who have this Spiritual treasure are like common clay pots, to show that the supreme power belongs to God, not to us. We are often troubled, but not crushed; sometimes in doubt, but never in despair; there are enemies, but we are never without a friend; and though badly hurt at times, we are not destroyed. At all times we carry in our mortal bodies the death of Jesus, so that His life also may be seen in our bodies. Throughout our lives we are always in danger of death for Jesus' sake, in order that His life may be seen in this mortal body of ours*". The confessions are painful stories yet we need to persevere because Jesus must be shown in us. We need sharp prayers and we need to stand firm beside our Master who in the end will bring all people and all creation to Himself.

Back in Malawi the Presbyterian Church is joining hands with the Church Universal in *Evangelism*. This Church celebrated its 1st 100 years in the country in 1976. Through *Evangelism* and *Renewal* programme, the Blantyre Synod will for the next 8 years be engaged in the Teaching Ministry. This will help lay a strong foundation in the faith and to help all

Christians to grow towards Spiritual maturity. To make this possible the Synod is engaged in intensive and extensive training of its personnel and all members of the Body of Christ starting from the little ones, the young to the elderly. We would like to train more of the nationals so that they can assume more responsibility in the Church than before. Already in the youth department, women's department and general administration all are headed by Malawians. While we aim at giving more and more responsibility to the indigenous people, we would like to maintain the universality of the Church. One way of doing this is the staff exchange programme under which I am here. Further we would like Church personnel here and some talented Christian friends to spend part of their Sabbatical leave working with us in Malawi. We need doctors and nurses to work at our Mission hospital in Mulanje. We need an architect to be in charge of a building department of the Synod, and we need secondary school teachers. Your service in Africa and particularly in Malawi will be a living testimony of the universality of the Church and the oneness of the people of God throughout the world.

Among you today, if you are wondering how best you can serve the Lord in His Church, this may be a chance for you to think about it seriously. I have left many questions unanswered deliberately. If what I have said has struck a cord let's meet privately and I will be delighted to discuss it with you.

(Preached in the USA, February 1977)

Appendix 5
Important Dates in the Life of Jonathan D. Sangaya

circa 1890   Mzangaya Dzonzi (Sangaya's father) takes refuge at Blantyre Mission.

31 October 1907   Jonathan Douglas Sangaya is born near Blantyre.

1913 Sangaya begins his education at Henry Henderson Institute (HHI) Primary School, Blantyre.

1924 Sangaya graduates from (the old) Standard Six.

1924-1926 Sangaya undergoes teacher training at Blantyre Mission.

1926 Sangaya receives the "English Grade Teacher" Certificate.

1926 Sangaya meets Christian Mtingala.

1927 Sangaya teaches Junior Primary School at Malabvi for one year.

1928 Sangaya is transferred to HHI Senior Primary School at Blantyre Mission.

1929 Jonathan Sangaya and Christian Mtingala are married by Rev. Harry Kambwiri Matecheta at St Michael and All Angels Church, Blantyre.

1930 Sangaya is promoted to School Supervisor (i.e. School Inspector).

1932 Lured by the prospect of earning more money, Sangaya leaves teaching and runs away to Zambia's copper belt. He spends only two months there however, before returning to Malawi that same year.

1939 War is declared in Europe.

1943 Sangaya joins the army and serves as an Education and Intelligence Officer in the King's African Rifles. He later achieves the rank of Warrant Officer - Class 2 - the highest rank that an African could achieve in the army.

1945 The war ends and Sangaya returns to HHI Primary School to take charge of the Junior Primary School.

1948 Sangaya joins the Theological College at Mulanje Mission.

1952 Sangaya graduates with a Certificate in Theology and is ordained the same year.

1952-1954 Sangaya serves as Assistant Minister to Rev. Harry Matecheta at Bemvu in Ntcheu.

1954-1959 Sangaya serves as Associate Minister at Blantyre Mission.

1959 Sangaya is appointed Assistant General Secretary of the Church of Central Africa Presbyterian, Blantyre Synod.

1961 Sangaya goes to Scotland to study church administration for one year.

1962 Sangaya becomes the first African General Secretary of Blantyre Synod CCAP.

1964 Malawi achieves independence under the leadership of Dr H. Kamuzu Banda.

1965 Utumiki Project started (Sangaya and Rev. Tom Colvin).

1967 Sangaya visits Christian Service projects in Ghana.

1968 Sangaya and Rev. T. Colvin form the Christian Service Committee (CSC) of the Churches in Malawi.

1978 Sangaya orders major repair work to be done on St Michael and All Angels Cathedral at Blantyre Mission.

22 July 1979 Sangaya dies.